THE WITTY WIDOW
By, Zoe Parkinson-Fisher

If you're reading this book, you either A) like a good laugh, whether it comes laughing with me or at me, or B) joined a club you wish you weren't a member of. I'm hoping you're reading this book for option A, but if it's for option B, I'm sorry girl, but you're in for a long, hard road (and not the long, hard we all need more of in our life). My name is Zoe Emily-Anne Parkinson-Fisher (yes, I'm a fan of hyphens), and I became a widow at 25 (in addition to an orphan at 22, but we'll dive into that hell-hole at a later time). So sit back, relax, pour a glass of wine (then drink the rest from the bottle), and enjoy the show.

A huge thank-you to everyone who
supported me throughout my first year of
widowhood and supported my dream to
make my story into a novel. Thank-you also
to all the wonderful women and men who
volunteered to read chapters from my book
and give me open and honest feedback.
Sharing my story definitely puts me in a very
vulnerable position, but without open and
honest communication, nothing will change.
If my story can save just one soul, I will
share it all. Your life matters. You are fierce.
We will fight this fight together. Always.

-Zoe

The Witty Widow

Prologue: A Few Words on Mental Health for Bell Let's Talk Day

(January 2018)

Bell Let's Talk Day is all about talking to raise awareness of and end the stigma surrounding mental health disorders. So let's talk. Let's talk about how mental illness has impacted every single one of your lives, believe it or not.

Right now; however, let's talk about how it's impacted my life. Because without talking there is no advocacy. There is no awareness. There is no change. There is no progress. Without talking there is no chance we can make a difference. There is no chance we can squash the negative stigma surrounding mental illness.

My dad lost his fight on September 10th, 2014. His demons grew to be too much and without proper medical intervention and counselling services, he lost his battle to depression. Sadly, he also took my mom with him. And believe it or not, my mother also suffered from anxiety herself. Two lives gone to mental illness.

My husband lost his fight on August 31st,

2017. He lost his fight to long-term depression and anxiety in the blink of an eye. My Quinn had sought treatment. He was taking medication and he had been to counselling in the past. But Quinn believed he could fight his battles with just medication alone and felt ashamed to go to counselling because "they didn't know anything anyway" and "people would judge him for going." However, research shows, the best way to treat mental illness is through a combination approach of medication paired with talk therapy. But the negative stigma surrounding this treatment pushed my husband away from the needed treatment, and he lost his battle after a long and hard fought war.

Here's my story. Long before my parents died, I struggled with anxiety. I slept little and worried for countless hours in university about "little things" and the panic attacks would strike when I'd get really sleep deprived and worked up over school or life. Then, my parents tragically died and the depression hit as well. I lost sleep, gained weight, and struggled to focus. Although I never sought out medication, I went to weekly therapy sessions to work through that trauma and get back to a healthy state of mind. About 2 years after their deaths, I think I got there. I was happy with the new life I had created with Quinn, proud of the career I had started for myself, and excited for what the future would hold for us. Quinn's own depression and anxiety appeared to be better too; he looked happier, was sleeping better, and was also talking about our future together.

In the blink of an eye, he was gone. Honestly, there have been times in the 8 years we were together that I thought he might take his own life. The day he actually died, was definitely not one of them. We've had some dark days, but he fought through every single one of them and worked hard to seek the help he needed and get "better." Depression; however, has no face and does not take into account how many wonderful things are happening in a persons' life at the moment it decides to take.

Quinn's death in a sense "ended his pain." But it is often said, when that pain ends for the person who dies by suicide, it spreads in waves to those around him. And it hit me hard.

Some days, I feel like life is good. Like I can conquer the world, and my universe wasn't shattered just 5 short months ago. I still laugh and joke and find joy in little things. I still strive to be fierce and do all things with love and kindness. Other days, when I least expect it, I can't breathe, and I can't think, and I can't feel anything but heavy and dark grief.

And the panic attacks hit. And not when I ever expect them to.

When I come home from work after a great day and want to share it with Quinn, the panic hits.

When I go to the grocery store to buy "real groceries" to try to cook for myself, the panic hits.

When I board a plane to go on vacation and realize I'm completely alone because my dog didn't board with me, the panic hits.

When I walk into a mall and see the crowds of people around me, holding hands and talking with their loved ones, the panics hits.

The panic just hits and I can't control it.

So why am I sharing this? Because stories like these need to be told. And I truly believe it is my job, my burden, my "cross to carry" to share this story. And to share it to bring awareness to mental health, and to show that it is ok to fall. It's ok to struggle. It's ok to have horribly awful bad days. But it's also ok to seek help. It's ok to take medication when you need to. It's ok to go to counselling. And hell, it's even ok to go to multiple counsellors. And it's sure as hell is ok to talk about your feelings, your fears, and your struggles. It's all just ok.

You are worthy of a good life. You deserve to find happiness. You are fierce. You are a fighter. And you will make it. It takes an army, and I will be standing next to you fighting in the front ranks beside you.

If you or someone you love is having suicidal thoughts or battling with mental illness, please reach out. You can save a life. You matter.

The Early Days

(November 2017)

I can remember the day the world turned black as if it happened just yesterday.

Ever felt like you've had déjà vu? The day my music died a second time is a day I will replay in my mind the rest of eternity. Yes, you read that correctly. Just 2 weeks shy of 3 years prior to this day I had received a call stating both my parents had passed away in a tragic mental health-inflicted tragedy. During this second bout of hell, I received another call telling me the one man who had been through every wonderful, beautiful, and soul-crushingly painful event with me perished in a very similar fate. My best friend, my childhood sweetheart, the love of my life, and my superman just couldn't fight his inner demons any longer and took his own life at the very young age of 25.

There he is.

Wasn't he a stunner? A solid 9.5 in my heavily biased, albeit very correct opinion. I was the definite let down in this relationship. I mean, how can you even compete? His crooked smile could light up a stadium. He radiated love, light, and warmth. And, do you know what? His soul was as breathtakingly gorgeous as his looks. He wasn't perfect, but he was damn close enough for me. And I loved every ounce of him. I loved him with all of my butt.

Yes, you read that correctly. I loved him with all of my butt, because my butt is a hell of a lot larger than my heart. I could honestly use a back-up cam to guide this rear-end around. But that's how much I loved him. With my entire ghetto booty.

My husband had been fighting a battle with depression and anxiety since long before we entered each other's lives. His family used to say one day he woke up and lost his smile, and it took years for him to find it again. Some of his family and friends told me after his death his smile returned when he fell in love with me, and others have said I gave him 8 extra years worth fighting for.

As a widow to a husband of suicide, let me tell you, hearing people say things like that are both comforting and outrageously painful. Hearing my love and his love for me kept him alive for all those years really made my heart feel full, but it also made me think what did I do to suddenly make that love not enough for him? Was it the not wearing makeup or dressing up to go out? Cooking gluten free? "Forgetting" to shave? Farting in bed? Gaining 20lbs to get a head-start on my future pregnancy weight?

Yes, I gave him 8 "extra" years, but I didn't give him 9. Or 10. Or the 60 he promised me when we married. If love could have saved him, he would have lived forever because, oh, did we love. But it wasn't enough. *Love wasn't enough.* I wasn't enough.

And I know you can tell me over and over it wasn't me. I didn't kill him. I couldn't have saved him. But these are the things I think about. How did I not see the signs? How did I not know that night he was going to do something so permanent? What did I do wrong in the days, weeks, or months leading up to his death that tipped him over the edge? Did I put too much pressure on him? Did I not tell him I loved him enough?

When did it all stop being enough? When did I stop being enough? When did love stop being enough?

If I knew the answer to these questions, I would have saved him.

But I didn't know the answers, and I still don't know the answers. Love just wasn't enough. Love failed us. The system failed us. I failed us.

In all seriousness, deep down I know I didn't cause the death of my husband, but when you live a life so intertwined and connected to someone, you can't help but wonder how the fuck you missed knowing he was so close to his breaking point.

Quinn's sister once said to me after his death, "Have you ever heard of suicide taking a horrible person? I think it only takes the best people." I couldn't agree more with that statement. I truly believe that those who die by suicide have such ridiculously big hearts and open souls that they spend all their time and energy holding everyone else up and building them up so they do not fall.

They do this so much that they themselves forget to reinforce and strengthen their own bodies and souls, so when they least expect it, they simply collapse. And no one's there to catch them, because no one saw the fault line. And you really can't see the fault line if it's covered by a vast and brave mountain, no matter how hard you search.

And trust me, I searched.

• • •

Those first few days following Quinn's death were nothing short of surreal. The day I found out Quinn had died, I honestly thought he was just asleep, because Quinn was the BEST sleeper I knew. I may or may not recall waking him up with a pail of water once, because I had given up on every other avenue and he was very, very late for work... sorry, babe. It was for your own good.

The day I knew he died I thought he was asleep because sleep made sense. Death definitely didn't. There was no indication for him to be dead. We had talked just two days prior and had a beautiful, short, sweet, and loving conversation, as two happily married people do. It wasn't a very notable conversation; in fact, it was very ordinary. We shared about our day, we shared about our plans for the next day, and we had a few laughs, said "I love you," and said "good night."

The week of his death was the week my sister had given birth to my beautiful blessing of a niece, Charlotte. Quinn and I had both driven down to Regina to meet our newest niece (and attend a kick-ass Guns 'n Roses concert), and then Quinn flew back to Calgary for the week to work. The plan was for him to come back Friday for the long weekend, so he could spend some more time with Charlotte and we could drive home together on Monday.

So on the day when I found out he was dead, I had no reason to worry until he didn't get off that plane. Quinn was notorious for sleeping in, and he was notorious for not checking his phone for long periods of time. I didn't hear from him for two days, but I didn't worry. I always worried about Quinn and for once I didn't want to let my irrational anxiety blow things out of proportion. So I kept telling myself he was fine: he was sleeping; he was going to get off that plane.

I didn't worry about Quinn that day. In fact, I didn't even tell my sister I hadn't heard from him until he was already supposed to be on that plane flying to Regina. And, do you know what I said to her when I told her this tidbit of information? I said, "If that idiot

The Witty Widow   *15*

isn't dead, I'll kill him myself for making me worry so much."

Yup, that's what I said, folks. I actually dropped the "d" word, as my husband was silently breathless back home.

Stupid, stupid word choice, Zoe.

When I did finally find out Quinn was dead, adrenaline kicked in hard. My body went into survival mode. It knew what to do. I had been through this before. The muscle memory my body created when I got the call of my parents passing kicked right back into high gear, and I put on my "business hat" and drove back to my sisters' house.

Yes, you read that right. I drove *myself* back.

I felt completely fine driving myself. My thoughts felt clear. I hadn't had time to process the emotions; I simply knew the facts and knew the steps I had to take before I could let myself succumb to the collapse of reality. The facts were my husband was dead: he was found by my neighbour and the police had called and confirmed it. The facts were the police now had Quinn's parents contact info and were going to call to confirm his death with them too, as I knew if they heard it from me it wouldn't quite be real; they needed the official call. The facts were I was stranded at an airport I didn't want to be at, and I had to get back to the remaining family I had, as there was nowhere else to go. The facts were there was a brand new baby in the house I was headed to, so I couldn't be the priority tonight. The facts were we needed help.

And, so I walked back into my sisters' house, still in survival mode. She hugged my emotionless body and told me she had called the aunts, and they were catching the first flight to Regina to take care of me here. And then she asked me who else I needed.

That's when I collapsed. That's when the emotion hit.

I no longer needed to take care of anyone else. I no longer was the caretaker. This time, I was the one who needed to be taken care of.

And, I collapsed.

In hours my best guy friend, Cody, was at Sarah's door. And I melted into his arms. This made it real. Two hours later, my aunts also walked through that door, in the middle of the night, to surround and comfort me.

I can remember not sleeping. Being told I needed to get some rest, but not processing any of it. I remember watching some weird show with my brother-in-law, Tyson, and Cody on how gold fish were produced, while my aunts whispered in the basement about the next steps that needed to be taken while Sarah rocked a colicky Charlotte back to sleep upstairs. And I remember being told I needed to try to sleep, but not being allowed to sleep alone for fear I might try to do something irrational to join Quinn that night.

The next day, still blurry, I knew I needed to inform Quinn's loved ones. My aunts offered to make the calls, but I knew I had to do them myself. One call after another, I could hear hearts breaking right over the phone. And each call I made, it became that much more real to me.

By noon, I was far from alone at that house. My three aunts, my sister, my brother-in-law, my new niece, my Cody, my Daikota, my Ashley, and my Hannah were all surrounding me. The remaining shreds of the family I was born into surrounding me, as well as the family Quinn and I had created were there. And, I didn't feel so alone.

And, as I sat there in my pyjamas, unshowered, with trails of yesterday's mascara streaking down my face from day-old tears, we began to share memories of Quinn. Every single memory shared was beautiful, happy, funny, and oh, so Quinn in every sense of the man. And we began to smile, to joke, and to laugh. Amidst all the hurt and tears; sorrow and agony; grief and confusion, we laughed. Because over the years of Quinn being in my life, he didn't just remain only "mine." No, over those 8 beautiful years we spent falling in love, he also became such a vibrant part of each and every person in that room's lives too. He morphed from acquaintance, to friend, and, finally, to family.

And, these people who loved me long before Quinn ever did, loved Quinn with the same fierceness they loved me with. He made a difference in their lives. He made their lives happy. He wasn't just a light in my life; he was also a light in every single person in that room's life, as well as so many more who weren't there that day. And, I honestly hadn't realized that until he wasn't there anymore. His absence in that room was so unbelievably apparent.

Sitting there in that room, surrounded by so many people who loved us, it suddenly dawned on me: I don't think Quinn realized how impactful he had been in all their lives either. I don't think he truly knew how much he was loved. Sitting there, all I could think about, was that Quinn was looking down on us all laughing, joking, and sharing our love for Quinn with each other, saying to himself, "Holy hell, I fucked up. I was **so** damn loved."

Because, babe, you really fucking were.

The days that followed were that of a blur. In the days, weeks, and even months that followed Quinn's death, I have very few memories of day-to-day events. I vaguely remember getting back to Calgary, walking into my empty house again for the first time and finding little clues of what happened leftover from the police and neighbours who tried to "rid" the house of any signs of death.

I remember seeing Quinn's family for the first time post-mortem and melting into them at the funeral home, apologizing all too many times for not being able to save their son. I remember seeing Quinn's motionless body at his viewing and screaming through tears as I held his cold face and begged him to come back to me, while his favourite band, The Red Hot Chilli Peppers, played in the background.

I remember picking up the urn of Quinn's ashes and waiting in my truck for my aunt to pop across the street to get us some tacos for the road back to Saskatchewan, while I took one last "family" photo with myself and the urn. I remember the eerie feeling of déjà vu as I walked into my Baba's house in Macklin and was flooded by hugs and tears from aunts, uncles, cousins, and friends, all waiting with heartbreak on their faces for me to arrive to do their best to show me I wasn't as alone as I felt in the world now.

But then it all starts to blur. I can see fragments of the funeral, the luncheon, the burial, and the drive back home. But I don't remember much for details. And once I got back to Cochrane, I honestly don't think I have a full memory of any part of any day until about Christmas. I mean, I know things about those months. The people that were there taking care of me have filled me in on some of their own memories of me during that time. But none of those memories are my own, and the time that I spent without anyone there, I have no recollection of at all.

The grief consumed me. It took hold of my body and sucked me in with one fierce swoop. The state I was in during those first few survival months is a state I find very hard to describe. It's a state of pure exhaustion, only you can never sleep. A state where you can go from crying to laughing to crying again in only a matter of seconds. A state where you forget how to move your limbs for even the most automatic of tasks, and hunger is a foreign feeling, which truly is mind-blowing to me as my cheeks are made primarily out of Doritos and mini eggs.

A state where you crave feeling any sort of emotion other than sorrow, so you make reckless and irresponsible decisions as often as you can just to try to get a rush of any sort of emotion possible. A state where even a small glass of red wine sends you straight into a psychotic breakdown and a blackout drunk that has you hallucinating your dead father is still alive and will fix everything, if only your best friend would dial the number you keep repeatedly screaming to him in tears as he tries to silence you and rock you to sleep...

A state that makes you question why you let your heart love someone so fiercely in the first place, if you were only going to lose that love in the end anyway....

But I clung to that love, and I survived each and every blurry day, until I didn't have to just survive them again. That love, Quinn's love, got me through it.

And, that shit head is going to have to wait 60 more years for me to tell him that, because I'm not joining him anytime soon. And, I plan on giving him one hell of a show while he waits for me.

The Story of Us

(September 2017 / April 2018)

I guess in order to really get to know my story and to get on the proper level needed to down a couple of bottles of wine while you read this book and shed full-on alligator sobs, you really need to know the story of our love. Allow me to share with you how it all began, grew, and blossomed into an eight-year, heart-stopping, stronger-than-death-itself love story filled with fierce passion, immense tragedy, and an extreme desire to make a life and build a new future together.

The story starts with two awkward, acne-ridden, and slightly funny-looking pre-adolescent children joining an after-school program known as Air Cadets.

Just kidding. Well, partially kidding.

We did meet in Air Cadets, but there was only one awkward, acne-ridden, and slightly funny-looking pre-adolescent child involved. Which would be me. The other pre-adolescent in this story was a handsome, blonde-haired, blue-eyed, smooth talker, who could wrap a lady around his finger in under a minute with that big crooked smile and smouldering look in his eyes. I met Quinn when I was 12. But I think he really only noticed me at 14, when I had gotten out of that awkward fat, boyish stage and wooed him over with my big brown eyes and witty lines. Even from the first day I met him, I had a serious crush on him. I would often say to my friends he was the popular, gorgeous guy who I would look at from afar but never have for myself. I told them it would take a true blue moon for me to get a guy like him.

Through cadets, Quinn and I soon learned we had many shared interests, and we became very close friends, growing into the best of friends. I often joked it took 6 long years to help "train" Quinn to be good boyfriend material before he finally worked up the nerve to ask me out. On January 1st, 2010 at the stroke of midnight, Quinn asked me out in the back of a barn. Ok, it was a Quonset. But barn just sounds so much better, so let's go with it. The temperature was -38C that night and, fittingly, there truly was a blue moon.

It's funny how one picture can tell so many stories within it.

This particular picture is the first picture of Quinn and I taken together as an official "couple." It was taken after we had come inside from freezing our asses off in the back of the barn and drank one or two too many "beazleys," or beer for anyone not from Cactus Lake out there, after I agreed to date Quinn. Sure, we'd taken pictures together before this date as friends, but this was the first photo of "Quinn and Zoe." The first photo where "me" became "we" (which by the way, changing pronouns has got to be one of the hardest things to accomplish).

This picture was taken on the night everything in our world would change. I don't think either one of us went into that night knowing this person we were about to say yes to being in a high school "relationship" with would grow to be the most important person in our life. Our other half. The one that made us laugh the hardest. The one that made us smile the biggest. And the one who taught us exactly how love should feel.

If I had known that night what would happen almost 8 years later, do I think my answer to Quinn's question would have changed? Would I have settled for a forever friendship and not let our bond turn into love? Would I have let him undo my jeans and have one passionate night together and then never talk to him again?

Who are we kidding with that last one. Everyone knows high school one-night-stands last all of 5 solid minutes with the guy throwing the girl a towel to "clean up" and the girl laying there with a very unsatisfied look on her face wondering if that was really what all the hype around sex was about.

Anyways, I digress.

If I would have known that very cold night in January that almost 8 years later the love of my life would be gone forever and my heart would break into millions of little fragments that could never fully be put back together, would I have still said yes to Quinn?

One thousand times yes. I'd say yes to Quinn any day of the week, wearing nothing but a paper bag in the middle of a crowd of nine thousand people. Any day, any time, anywhere. My answer would always be yes.

I would say yes because the 8 years I felt Quinn's love were the best 8 years of my life. The most full years of my life. Full of laughter; full of care; full of support; full of pleasure (and full of sex); full of understanding; full of respect; and most importantly, full of pure, passionate, unfiltered, non-judgmental love. And what is life without love?

Quinn taught me so many incredible lessons through the 8 years we were together. Sure, I could go on and on and tell you detail by detail about how our lives unfolded in those 8 years. How I went off to school and he called me every single day (minus 3 days) for the 6 years I was in a different country studying to be a speech-language pathologist. I could tell you about how Quinn stuck by my side during a horrible car accident and again during the then biggest tragedy of my life, when my father killed my mother and then himself and Quinn was the unfortunate person to find the bodies. I could tell you about how Quinn fumbled in his suitcase for almost 5 minutes while he was down on one knee and trying to propose when he came to visit me at university a month after my parents died (of course I said yes before he could even fully get the words out). And, I could tell you all about our fairy-tale wedding in Jasper, Alberta with mountains and bears, family and friends, and of course our beautiful furbaby, Layla, who was, of course, the star of the show. I could tell you about all the hard moments, the moments where we struggled to make our relationship work and had to learn about true forgiveness, communication, respect, and trust in order to overcome those darker moments we faced.

I could go on and on about every little moment in life we shared together. But those memories are for me and those memories are for him. I'll keep those memories safe in little boxes along shelves piled up in my brain. Anytime I need a reminder of that deep and wonderful love we shared, I can simply pull down a box from my shelf and replay that beautiful memory in my mind over and over and over again, or share it with someone I love, until I can hear his voice ringing in my ears, feel his touch against my skin, and see his smiling face looking right into my soul.

Because, we loved.

We really, truly, honestly, and fully loved. And I wouldn't give up that love, no matter how short it lasted on earth, for the entire world. Because the strength of the love we shared was and is so much stronger than death. It truly was and is a love that has no end. A love that will go with me to my grave. A love that will give me strength in my darkest of days to guide me to carry on and continue searching for the good. A love that I will learn to love myself with first, and then love others with one day as I slowly open my heart, lower my walls, and begin to let people in again. A love that I will base every other relationship I have on, and

The Witty Widow   29

although I know no man will ever love me the way Quinn did, I will know that love is out there and that the new man who walks into my life one day will love me exactly the way he can. And it will be a different love, but it will be a good love. And it will never alter the love that Quinn and I shared and will always share. Because, true love never dies.

And, oh hot damn, was our love true.

So You're Going to a Funeral

(Written piece by piece throughout the year)

Life comes with death. And guaranteed, we're all going to get a phone call, read a text message, or see a post on social media sharing someone we knew and loved took their last breath and departed our world. It's life, and we all know one day or another, death is sure to follow.

But how do you act at a funeral? What is helpful or not helpful? Is there a certain social code (oh shit, out comes the speech-language pathologist in me) for comforting grievers of different forms of grief? What is expected? What is the "norm?" Should you talk about the person who died or avoid the topic all together? Is it cool to throw at the griever your own religious beliefs or should you avoid the dreaded faith debate all together? What cliché phrases should you say to the grieving loved ones to try to boost their spirits in their darkest moments? Should you get them flowers and bring them 3 meat trays, 2 fruit trays, and a Costco-size bag of buns?

I get asked these questions quite frequently, as in recent years I've become somewhat of an expert on funerals. A title I've never wanted to have but "lucked out" into getting. And by "lucked out," what I really mean is life throat punched me, turned me over to dust me off, then gave me a solid kick in the teeth for good measure. And now here I am, a funeral expert.

Bringing Over Gifts

When someone you know has died, the first thing many people think is "what can I do to help the survivors while they grieve?" Giving gifts is a simple thing anyone can do, whether they know the family very well or are a concerned acquaintance, which really goes a long way in showing the grieving individuals someone out there cares and is there.

But what exactly is a good gift to give a griever? What will they actually use and not just toss away?

- Fruit and Vegetable Trays-
  You can never go wrong with a SMALL fruit or veggie tray. When grief hits, often you can barely remember to eat, so it is sure nice to have something easy (and healthy) to

just pop in your mouth without any thought or effort required. I say small, as these trays often expire quite quickly and if 10 people all bring one over, a lot goes to waste.

Although fruit and veggie trays are wonderful, I can honestly say I NEVER want to see another meat or cheese tray in my life. I actually think I suffer some PTSD from the amount of meat and cheese I ingested the week after my parents died. Please, for the love of all that is good, refrain from buying the jumbo-sized meat tray. Ten others will do the same, and the family will have nightmares of rolled ham and turkey for months. It's been over 4 years, and to this day, I have and will not touch a meat or cheese tray.

- Toilet Paper-

    Often when a loved one dies you end up having a hundred people trooping through your home to care for and comfort you. The last thing running through your mind is, "are we good on toilet paper?" When my parents died, some of my friends brought this over, and it proved to be the most useful gift.

- Paper Towel, Paper Plates, Disposable Cutlery, Napkins-

  Basically anything disposable that will make the person's life easier. And yes, I'm aware it's not good for the environment, but when the world shatters and you can barely focus on getting dressed let's focus on saving the planet next month instead. The griever will have no energy to clean once you leave, so let's make their life as simple as possible.

- Individual Freezer Meals-
  Seriously, such a lifesaver after a death. When Quinn died, a remarkable person (whom I didn't even know very well at the time) came over and brought a cooler full of individual freezer meals for me. Talk about a lifesaver. After Quinn's death, I barely had the energy to shower, let alone eat, and I can tell you point-blank there wasn't even a shred of energy left in me to cook anything. The freezer meals made it so at least I could pop the bag into the microwave and have one meal a day that didn't involve chocolate or wine, even though, we all know chocolate and wine make for the most balanced of meals and should be a part of your daily nutrition.

- Bringing Over Supper-

   But always asking the grievers in advance if it's ok and when would be a useful day to bring over a meal. Often everyone brings food at once and a lot of it goes to waste. Checking in advance with the grieving family to make sure there isn't too much food already is most helpful. It's also helpful to remember that after the funeral, the grief doesn't stop. So waiting until a week or two after the funeral before offering to bring a meal is a great idea.

   I remember very vividly, about a week after my parents' deaths, Quinn's boss brought over two rotisserie chickens and all the fixings. Quinn and I were so unbelievably tired of "funeral food" (i.e. meat and cheese trays), so we each flopped down on a couch in our living room with a chicken on our stomachs and ate the entire chickens straight from the containers. It seriously was the most delicious chicken meal of my life.

- Gift certificates for Food or Pampering-
   Such thoughtful and wonderful gifts. It was so nice knowing we could order a

meal anytime after the funeral and it would be covered or to be able to de-stress with a massage or mani/pedi and not think of the costs on top of the funeral costs and estate planning.

- A "Feel Good" Gift Basket-
Motivational quotes, chocolate, bubble bath, teddy bears, colouring books, slinkies, slime balls... whatever silly and fun gift you can think of (even from the dollar store) will brighten the griever's life. Just a little ray of sunshine to lighten the mood can mean the world to the griever. It truly doesn't have to be anything more than a pack of gum or a favourite chocolate bar, with a little "I'm thinking of you" note attached.

- Individual Packs of Kleenex-
Because, at least with me, I could have replenished the Atlantic Ocean with the amount of tears I cried in the first few weeks. It was nice to have an unending supply of tissues on hand.

- Leaving a Gift on the Step-
Ok, this isn't exactly a specific gift, but I found it incredibly thoughtful and wonderful to not have to answer the door to person after person when

Quinn died. Yes, it was so thoughtful for friends and neighbours to bring gifts or come to visit, but honestly, I had no energy to visit with anyone and just wanted to cry and sleep. Those that respected my privacy and left their gifts on my porch instead of ringing the doorbell helped me so unbelievably much, as I had terrible anxiety answering the door and would become quite panicked every time that doorbell rang in the first few months.

Funeral Etiquette

So what exactly is your role when you get to the funeral? You go to support the grieving family and to show your love and respect for the soul lost, but when does too much support become too much?

Here are some quick Do's and Don'ts to attending a funeral:

Don't:

- Go to a funeral if you don't personally know the deceased or his or her immediate survivors. Sometimes too many people is just that, too many. Please never go to a funeral to "watch the show" and say you were there.

- Line up to hug the survivors if you are not a dear loved one of theirs. My ribs hurt for THREE days after Quinn's funeral, and I've completely blacked out any recollection of the hundreds-long hugging line at my parents funeral. That amount of sweat, tears, consolation, and smudged makeup was traumatic to say the least. If you've never hugged me before, that day is not the day to start.

- Bombard the griever's home. After a traumatic death, or any death for that matter, the surviving grievers are exhausted; stressed; grief-stricken. Yes, they need to know there is support around them and people to help pick up the pieces, but not all at once. Always ask first before coming, respect the individuals' privacy, don't overstay your welcome, and never expect to be waited on like a guest during this visit. Short and sweet are wise words to put into practice in this scenario. |

Do:

- Sign the guestbook to let the family know you're there for support and to pay your respects to the deceased. Signing the book or leaving a card is so much more helpful than an unfamiliar hug.

- Donate to a charity selected by the family in their loved one's honour if you'd like to do something for the family. This donation makes a more lasting impact on the family, community, and society than flowers or a card. It shows you care and want to fight the fight with the family.

- Share a story about the deceased with the family, whether it's at the funeral, in a card, or at a later date. Talking about the loved one lost keeps their memory alive, which validates to those grieving that their loved one was alive, loved, and will be remembered. You have no idea how much it means to me when someone unexpectedly shares a story about my husband, dad, or mom. It puts my heart at so much ease knowing I'm not the only one who still thinks about them. And for the short time their story is being shared, it feels

like they're still here, which truly is a
beautiful thing.

- Keep things light. Remember humour
  can be some of the best medicine, if
  used appropriately (if you know the
  grievers, you'll know what's
  appropriate). Remember, not all
  grievers are quite as witty as this
  widow.

Honestly, the best part of my
husband's funeral was when one of his
old neighbours pulled me aside and
told me he had something very
important he needed to show me on his
phone that he thought Quinn's dad and
I would fight over. I assumed he would
show me a nice photo of Quinn, but
instead he pulled up a photo of a very
large cucumber from his garden. You
have no idea how wonderful seeing
that photo of a cucumber was. It gave
me a break from reality, a laugh, and
showed me just how much the
neighbour actually cared for Quinn and
our family. He understood grief and
loss, as he was a widower as well, and
knew I needed a bit of a reprieve from
all the sadness. So thank-you, thank-
you, thank-you, dear neighbour. That
was the one light memory I have from

that day, and oh, did I need that lightness.

To Say or Not to Say

I swear I've heard it all. It has never ceased to amaze me what comes out of people's mouths when they hear of someone's death and try to speak to the loved one. Notice how I said "speak to" and not comfort? Because I honestly believe not everything said to the grieving loved ones is always meant to comfort them. Sometimes, I think what is said is more to comfort the person speaking, to help them find some closure and peace by checking in with the griever or unloading their own thoughts, feelings, and opinions on them.

The biggest tip I would give people trying to speak with a grieving loved one is to remember the phrase "one size fits all."
Got that phrase in your head?

Now knock it out with a baseball bat, because, my dear friends, one phrase does not fit all when it comes to death.

Wow, Zoe. That was a bit harsh, yes? Maybe, but let me explain what I mean.

Each death is very different. The death of a 90-year-old grandfather who died in his sleep after living a long and happy life surrounded by a big, loving family is a much different death than that of a 21-year-old youth who lost her battle to cancer. The first death is in many ways a celebration of a long life well-lived. The second, a tragedy of a pained life lost much too soon. In the first situation, a phrase such as "He lived a great and full life" would be very fitting. Not so much, with the second situation for obvious reasons above and beyond the second death being that of a female (insert laughter here…).

As with the above example, some phrases commonly used to express sympathy and/or empathy definitely do not apply to every death. Specifically, to a tragic and unexpected death. Some of the phrases I found most difficult to hear included (but were far from limited to):

- "He's in a better place right now." Really? So you're saying death is a better scenario than married life with me?

- "I'm sorry for your loss." Yes, I know this phrase is just someone expressing how sad they are for you, but when my parents died, I found this phrase infuriating. Why are you sorry? To be sorry implies you've done something wrong. The last time I checked, you didn't kill my loved ones. So why are you sorry again?

- "You should get some sleep, you look exhausted." No shit, Sherlock. The sudden death of my husband actually makes me sleep like a baby. In fact, I've never felt better.

Please note the heavy amounts of sarcasm I'm using here. In the months following my husband's death, the only sleep I got was when someone told me I had to watch their favourite movie and proceeded to turn it on. Instant coma.

I knew I looked like death. I didn't need anyone pointing that fact out to me. And telling a fresh widow to try to get some sleep is like telling a newborn to start walking. It doesn't happen instantly but rather requires months of growth to work yourself up to sleeping soundly alone.

Additionally, the beliefs of the griever should also be taken into consideration when trying to console a griever with your words. I understand that many people find great comfort in their own religious beliefs and in believing their loved ones are now being cared for by a higher power. If it helps you sleep at night, by all means, continue believing in your higher power. But please, always remember the griever you are trying to comfort may not in fact have the same beliefs as you, and the words you are saying to try to give them comfort and peace might instead bring heartache and pain.

I was raised Catholic. My mom took us to church every Sunday, and my dad, although he had no religious beliefs of his own, supported the decision to raise us as Catholics and showed up for the "big events" at church (i.e. Holy Communion, Christmas, Easter) from time to time.

I've never had a firm belief in the Catholic idea of God; however, I've always believed in some form of a higher power. When my parents died the way they did; however, my beliefs were completely shattered. How could a loving and all-powerful God destroy lives like he just did? After Quinn's death, I was done. Any last shred of faith flew out the window. There in no God, in my eyes, who thinks its ok to destroy someone's life, let them shake it off for a couple years, then destroy it a second time. Please don't tell me it's a test of my faith. Please don't tell me it is part of a bigger plan, because if I had plans like that at my job I'd be fired instantly. To me, it's just all kinds of awful. And, if I'm wrong and there is a God out there, please, please, please, enlighten me on this "bigger plan" you have. I am dying to know what wonderful things you have in store for me.

Personally, I believe life is a series of choices. I believe we choose the path we are on, and we choose how we respond to the events that define our lives. I believe in spirits, but I don't believe in an all-powerful God. I believe my loved ones are always surrounding me and, call me crazy if you want, but I do believe I can feel them with me from time to time. Something funny happens, and I swear I hear my mom's laugh. My car door won't open, and I know my dad is messing with the locks, as he always enjoyed causing trouble and was known to be a bit of a shit-disturber. I come home from a trying day, and I feel Quinn's lips on my forehead.

My point is, not everyone believes what you believe. And when someone dies, emotions are high and people are questioning sometimes already shaky or non-existent belief systems. Being told "everything happens for a reason" or "this is part of God's plan" may be comforting to someone with a strong belief in God or someone who has not been through the traumatic death of a loved one, but from personal experience it had the opposite impact on me. The priest who presided over Quinn's funeral service, for example, was very lucky my dominant wrist was in a splint because when he told me Quinn's death was part of God's bigger plan, the only thing I wanted to do was give him a black eye and ask him if that was also part of God's genius plan.

Here are a few more miscellaneous gems I've had thrown at me after the death of my husband, which have since given me a good laugh although many of them hurt like hell when said. I hope they give you a good laugh too. I also hope reading them makes you realize how vastly inappropriate many of these quotes were to say to a newly grieving widow. Enjoy.

- "I know how you are feeling right now…" because I'm going through a divorce.

No. Just, no.

You cannot relate a divorce to a death of a spouse. I loved my husband. I had a good marriage with him. We still wanted to be married. Additionally, you still have the option to see your spouse. You still have the option to scream at him, hit him, or beg him to come back. You still have the possibility of making things work and being with him again.

I have none of that. So please, never try to tell me you know how I feel.

- Just two weeks following Quinn's funeral, I got a message on social media from a man from Quinn's home town whom I didn't know well, but knew of. He was asking me how I was doing, so I assumed he must have once been a friend of Quinn's and was reaching out to see how his grieving widow was doing. This man then proceeded to ask if I'd like to get a coffee with him sometime because, wait for it, I had "nice eyes" at the funeral.

I guess tears bring out the brown?

- Just two months after my husband died, my Dyido (or grandpa for you non-Ukrainians), also passed away. At the prayer service the night before his funeral, an elderly second cousin of mine came up to me, gave me a very large and lingering hug, and whispered in my ear "I so wish you were pregnant right now...."
  After I heard this little gem, I popped a large Ativan, went down to the bar, and got good and drunk. Because non-pregnant widows have the option to do that.

A word of wisdom: Never, ever express your opinion to a widow on whether or not she is better off with or without children. You don't know what's going through her mind. Your opinion or "advice," no matter which side you take, will only make her feel worse. So just keep your moth shut and avoid the child topic all together.

- My two oldest nieces had exceptionally different perspectives of Quinn's death and definitely weren't shy to share those perspectives with their Auntie Zoe. The younger of the two who was 4 at the time told me when she missed her Uncle Quinn, she just looked outside and found the brightest star in the sky, and she knew that star was him shining down on her. Her older sister who was then 6, had a much more logical perspective on Quinn's death. She told me I should wear all his clothes and use all his stuff because, well, he was dead anyway.

- On that same note, my 4-year-old niece was sitting on my lap at a benefit concert Quinn's parents were playing at to raise money for mental health awareness about 6 months after Quinn died. This little sweetheart saw her Auntie Zoe crying and wanted to make things better for me so she said, with a look of pure genius in her eyes, "Auntie, I know how we can fix this… you can just find me a new uncle!" If only it was that easy, sweetheart.

Delusional Days

(March 2018)

"It's only before realities set in that we can treasure our delusions." – Anna Quindlen

Delusions are often symptomatic of a mental disorder. Well folks, I must have crazy written all over me because some days I bathe in my delusions.

I love talking to strangers for that reason alone. Why do you think my nails always look fierce? Why are my brows chronically on-point? Because, in the hour it takes for women to want to be me and men to want to be with me (come on, you know I just tell it how it is), I get to pretend my life is perfect. I get to pretend my husband is at work and he's not really a fan of glitter polish, so maybe I'll just stick to neutral shellac today. I get to pretend that I've been happily married to my high school sweetheart for almost two years, and we're crossing our fingers this is the month we find out we're expecting. I just get to pretend everything is made up of sunshine and butterflies and the world is a perfect place.

And you know what?

I fucking love pretending.

Even when I'm not talking to strangers, I find myself diving into delusions that Quinn is here. I find myself playing scenarios in my head of what he would say or what he would do if he were here right now. "Hunny, can you grab me a towel? I'm in the tub and can't reach." "Quinnee, can we go to the mountains just one more time this weekend? I feel bears in my bones." "Babe, I'm not making you a sandwich. Sandwich making was not part of our vows." "Stop pinching my butt you shithead. If I fall down the stairs one more time, you may learn what runs in my family." Murder. Murder, apparently, runs in my family.

Sometimes I can hear his responses back clear as day. I can hear his evil laughter as he pinches my butt yet another time. I can see him smiling away, the biggest shit-grin you'd ever see, as he continually does and says everything he can think of to annoy me just a little bit more so I'll snap and he can laugh at how funny "mad Zoe" is.

I can hear him playing "Walk this Way" and "Sweet Child O' Mine" on his guitar as he sips his morning coffee at the kitchen island. I can hear him changing keys over and over until it's in the perfect key for me to sing along to "Chances Are" with him, which by the way was the only country song I'd sing with him, because I simply love Gwyneth

The Witty Widow 51

Paltrow and Country Strong was a bomb movie. I must have been crazy back then too, because as we sang I would imagine our kids sitting at the kitchen table eating breakfast, watching Daddy play, listening to Mommy sing, and thinking to themselves, "Wow, this is what real love is meant to look like."

Sometimes I can still feel my legs laying on top of his as we watch TV on the couch; I can still feel the warmth of his lips and taste the salt of his skin as he kisses my lips and then my forehead, as only someone who truly loves you would; I can feel the rhythm of our feet as we dance to Ed Sheeran in the living room; I can even smell his scent, as if I'm wrapped up in his arms and everything is perfectly right in the world. Those are the best days. Those are the worst days. Those days are my reality.

And, sometimes, I imagine he's still dead. But that he left me the one gift I had been wanting for many years until he finally said he was ready and wanted to try too.

Sometimes, I make believe soon after Quinn died I realized I was pregnant. I pretend I didn't have to walk this world without him with me because a piece of him would always be in our baby. Sometimes I pretend the 14lbs I gained following his death was actually 30lbs of baby weight, and I was

ery ready; patiently
st gift Quinn could
ys I pretend that baby
Quinn promise if we
me name her this)
me a true purpose to

....s someone I could
share Quinn with. Someone who wanted to
hear every single story about his childhood.
Someone who wanted to know exactly how
Mommy met Daddy, and why it took 6 years
for Daddy to ask Mommy out in the first
place. Someone who could snuggle in with
Mommy as she cried from missing Daddy
ridiculously hard and would help make
birthdays and holidays special again so
Mommy felt something other than gut-
wrenching pain when others were singing
festive songs and decorating their homes
with love and laughter. Someone Mommy
would have with her so people would stop
telling her "well at least you two didn't have
children" or "the good part is, since there's
no kids, you can start a fresh life." Because,
again folks, neither of these things said have
ever been and will never be helpful to a
grieving young widow. No matter how witty
she is.

And, you know, even though I have these
delusional moments, I know they are just

The Witty Widow   *53*

that, delusional moments. I know Quinn is gone. I know I'm not pregnant and will never be pregnant with his baby. I know I'm still up 14lbs and my thighs have become best friends because they're now closer than ever. I know what my reality is no matter how hard I wish it wasn't my reality.

But, do you know what else? I think these delusional moments are rather healthy. I think these delusional moments give me reprieve when my mind can't process he's actually gone. I think these delusions help calm me when panic strikes and I feel the world about to crash around me. I think living in the beautiful moments we had together and picturing the beautiful life we were meant to live together is perfectly normal and perfectly ok. And, I think that tricking my brain into believing these false realities for a few moments allows me to continue to put one foot in front of the other, because the reality is my once thought of reality no longer exists. My once thought of future can no longer unfold. Every single life plan I had ever made vanished into thin air the moment I heard Quinn had stopped breathing.

And, that is what nightmares are made of.

So, I will continue to find retreat in my delusions and I will continue to be that crazy young widow who talks about her husband to any random stranger that will listen as if he never lost his battle. As if he never left my side.

Because that is how I survive. And I'm ok with that.

Photos and Memories

(June 2018)

Photographs, in my opinion, were the best invention on earth. With the single click of a camera (or touch on a smartphone), you've just captured a single memory forever in the rawest of forms. I live through photographs now and probably spend more time looking at those photos and relieving those memories than I do making new ones. How grateful I am that my mom walked around with a camera attached to her hand at all times. How grateful I am that when my mom passed, I too morphed into that crazy camera lady and spent a lot of time making Quinn pose for selfies and action shots with me.

Photos can be so beautiful and pull you into such incredible memories, creating feelings of warmth, love, and comfort around you, but they can also be incredibly difficult to look at. They can be reminders of all the love, life, and happiness that was lost.

When Quinn died, this was how I felt about photos of him in my house. I found it incredibly difficult to walk around my home and see harsh reminders of his death in every photo I had of him. I had pictures of us in the kitchen, living room, office, basement, hallways, and in our bedroom. These pictures just got to be far too much for me, and about a month after he died, I had enough and took them down. I needed him gone. I needed photos of him gone. I needed the reminders of the happiness we once had gone. It was just too hard. It was just too much to look at his beautiful, handsome, loving, and happy face. Just far too much.

So, I packed up all our beautiful photographs and memories, put them into boxes, and closed the lids tight. The only photographs I left up were a couple in our bedroom that I couldn't quite bare to part with just yet. I also left his funeral card up on my fridge door, which I think I kept there as a grounding reminder of the reality I now faced every day. To this day, it still hangs on that fridge. I've not yet had the strength to take it down, and truthfully, I'm not sure I ever will.

Taking down the photos in my house has caused some controversy in opinions from my friends and family I've had to listen to. Some family members told me not to rush taking them down and that if I took them down too early, I'd regret it in the future. Others told me I should box up every single thing that reminded me of Quinn and start fresh to symbolize moving on and birthing a new life for myself.

I still remember my then 4-year-old niece coming over to my home a few months after her Uncle Quinn died and asking me why I didn't have any photos of him up in the house anymore. I responded to her by saying the photos of Uncle Quinn made Auntie Zoe's heart hurt because Auntie missed Uncle so much so she had put them away in a safe place to look at when she was strong again. My little sweet niece, who I'm so sure will find her calling in a helping profession one day, looked at me and said very innocently, "Auntie, for Christmas I'm going to get you every single picture of Uncle Quinn to hang up in your home." Oh please, hunny, no. Auntie's heart would break into a million little pieces if she got a gift like that. No matter how beautiful it would be, it would just hurt like hell.

After removing the photos of Quinn from my own house, I began to notice in a number of my friends and family's houses, more and more photos of Quinn were appearing. It was almost like his death had the opposite effect on them; like they needed reminders of the memories they had with him, and they could accomplish that by adding photos of him.

Now, not everyone I knew did this. My sister and my grandma were similar to me and found it very difficult to see his face every day, so they too had taken a lot of photos down. But others, particularly Quinn's immediate family and some of my aunts, uncles, and friends, actually began putting photos of Quinn up in their homes where there hadn't been any photos of him before.

I spoke about this to my counsellor during a recent counselling session. She asked if I had photos of Quinn in my home, and I shared with her how I removed them shortly after his death. I also talked with her about how others had put more photos of him up in their homes. My counsellor then asked me why I thought I had done the opposite and took photos down versus putting more up. I thought for a bit about this question and then responded to my counsellor.

You see, I didn't need photos of Quinn up in my house because Quinn was everywhere in my home. I look at the kitchen island and see him sitting there playing guitar as he drinks his morning coffee. I look to my left as I sit on the couch and see him laying down beside me eating a bag of peanuts and drinking a beer. I roll over in bed and see him sleeping peacefully beside me and I so badly want to wake him in a very fun way and let him do very fun things to me. I look out the back window and see him mowing the lawn. Everywhere I look, I close my eyes and the memories of Quinn flood in. I don't need a photo to have Quinn in my house. My house became my home because Quinn was in it. Photos don't change that. He's already here.

There's a song by Joshua Moss called "House" that goes, "This house is hard without you here. It's a lot less like home. The little things have disappeared and the places you'd sit are everywhere."

Have a listen to it. It's a beautiful song and hits the nail on the head regarding how I feel about my house now that Quinn is no longer in it. Physically, he's gone, but in memories he's in every single corner. And, although I tell everyone I love my house and feel it still is my home, it's definitely become a lot less like home without Quinn here. The thing I loved most about my house was who I shared it with and now that love is gone.

Quinn was a part of my everyday. Every single day for 8 years I saw his smiling face, felt his loving touch, or heard his deep, soothing voice. He was my reality and part of every memory I had for 8 years. His family and friends didn't have him like I did. He wasn't part of their every day, although I know he was a huge part of their lives too. So adding those photos of Quinn to their homes brought him back into their memories and reminded them of the happiness they shared with him. That's what helped them to cope with his loss and keep him alive. And that, although different than my own actions, is simply beautiful as well.

This photo, this picture right here, is my favourite photo in the entire world.

Why, you might ask?

Because in this moment, in this exact moment captured, every single thing was completely perfect in my world. I had two loving and incredibly supportive parents cheering me on. I had a family that wasn't separated by grief and trauma and unanswered questions. I had a loving and devoted man in my life I knew I could count on. I had high grades and low worries. I ran everyday and looked as good as I felt. I was vibrant, happy, and full of so much life. I had everything. Every single little thing in my world was right. It was good. It was just as I imagined my life to be. I had everything.

And, then I had nothing. Mental illness took it all from me in the blink of an eye. One moment, life was great, and the next, it just wasn't. Depression slaughtered my mom and destroyed my dad. And, then, just when I was feeling safe and secure again, it came back with a vengeance and ripped the love of my life out of my arms, without a second thought.

Depression didn't stop to consider if I had been through enough trauma yet. It didn't stop to look at the last few months and decide to give the newly weds a few years to settle down and start a life together. It didn't stop to consider the plans we had made for the future. No, depression has no face; it has no filter; and it takes when it pleases. And, trust me, it takes. It is a very real and very damaging disease that can become fatal at any moment if left untreated. It doesn't look at what's fair, or right, or just when it takes. It just takes.

And, can I tell you a secret?

Some days, I'm fucking terrified it's going to take me too. I'm terrified one day I won't be able to handle the trauma, the grief, the reality, or the loneliness anymore, and it will be sitting at my door too, just waiting for its moment to come take me as well. It's waiting. It's always waiting. And I'm never sure if I'll have enough tools in my toolbox to fight it forever. What if the cycle never stops?

Now I know what some of you are thinking, "Oh goodness, Zoe's suicidal, sound the alarms and alert the media. Get her help, get her help, now."

Breathe. Just breathe.

I'm not suicidal. I don't think about dying or ending my pain, although finding a way to end the hurt in my heart would be wonderful a lot of the time. The ending to that hurt I'm looking for; however, doesn't involve anything as close to the permanence of death. It involves finding new light, finding new life, and one day, when I'm ready, hopefully finding new love.

I am a fighter; I am a warrior; I am fierce; and you won't get rid of me anytime soon.

Looking Into the Future

(December 2017)

So what does the future hold for an orphaned, childless, widow you may ask? Tacos. Lots and lots of tacos. And wine. Not by the bottle but by the barrel.

Apart from that, I'm not too sure what my future holds. Not too long after Quinn's death, I had a counselling session with my grief counsellor, and I spoke with her about Quinn's loss being so much more than just the loss of a husband. I spoke to her about how close Quinn was to my parents and how he would be the only man who ever got to know them, be loved by them, and get their blessing for marriage, although he never had the chance to physically ask them before they passed. I also spoke with her and stated that the loss of Quinn meant the loss of future babies together, as we had been trying for 3 months to start a family. I had never been so excited in my life as I was thinking about the prospect of being a mother to Quinn's children.

Once I had said this to my counsellor she took a very long pause, breathed a big, deep breath, and said, "Well, it seems to me the death of your husband is not only the death of your past…but also the death of your future."

That's it.

That's all she said.

She didn't say it was "the death of the future you planned." She didn't say, "it was the death of the future you thought but now it was up to you to create a new future." She simply said, "It was the death of your future."

Talk about a warm fuzzy moment right there. Moments like those are the moments where you feel like you're hugging a rotting bag of feces while dangling over a pit of alligators wearing nothing but a pair of parachute panties. A true feel-good family moment.

In all seriousness, I think the hardest part of moving on in a future relationship without Quinn will be just that; it will be without Quinn. I've spoken with a few of my friends and family about this particular realization, and find it to be the hardest one I've come to yet. When, and if, I meet a truly amazing guy who checks all my boxes (in and out of the bedroom) and makes me scream daily (only in the bedroom), and we make beautiful babies together, I'll be able to share with my new family and babies memories of my parents. I'll be able to put their pictures up in their nurseries and talk to them about how much Grandad and Grandma would have loved them, tell them stories about what they were like growing up and the adventures they went on together and took my sister and me on, and eventually, when they are old and have grown a little tough from life, I will share with them how mental illness tragically took them away from us all too soon.

But I won't be able to do that with Quinn. Quinn won't be an important figure in their lives. He won't be an uncle or a friend or a grandpa. He won't be a dad. They won't want to hear stories about his childhood. They won't want to hear how Mommy fell in love with him in the back of a barn on a freeze-your-ass-off -38C New Years Eve. They won't want to hear how Quinn called Mommy in Minot every single day (-3 days) for 6 years while they were apart because, well, he had promised her he would. They won't want to hear of their fairy tale wedding in Jasper or of their exotic honeymoon in Tenerife, Spain, off the coast of Africa sipping mojitos and singing along to Chocolatte (Choco-choco-la-la.... Everybody say Chocolatte- YouTube it. I dare you to. Say goodbye to having any other song in your head for the next 3 months).

They won't want to hear about his long and hard-fought battle with mental illness that ultimately took his courageous and strong soul all too soon. They won't want to visit his grave with Mommy and cry beside Mommy as she lays flowers on his headstone and dreams of a whole other life with this other man they knew nothing of and have no interest in knowing of. Because he's not their daddy. He's just a man who loved their mom long before their daddy came to be. In their little world, he's nothing. There will never be little Quinns running around ready to hear and pass on his memories to future generations.

His story ends with me.

And, that, my friends, makes for one hell of a great country song. Maybe I'll have to take up writing country music for my next side project. Let's face it, the material I have is solid gold. Bring on the twang.

Sometimes, You've Just Got to Laugh

(September 2018)

Caution: This chapter is not for the easily offended. If you fit into that category, I encourage you to flip to the next chapter. My comedic genius has no censor in this chapter, and my high school nickname "Potty-Mouth Parkinson" definitely has earned its merit over the last year. So, if you can handle a few politically incorrect jokes, please proceed.

My dad always said, "If you don't laugh, you go crazy." This motto, I have clung to all year long. I firmly believe if I didn't have such a witty sense of humour, I would have fallen apart months ago. Probably years ago when the first fist smacked me across my face.

Literally, the day after Quinn died, the jokes started flowing. I know, when you're husband kills himself you're not supposed to immediately resort to funny jokes about dating with urns or how ashy you're husband is looking lately, but what else do you do? It's either you cry until your tear ducts block and your head pounds like a sex addict going to Vegas after a year of abstinence, or you laugh until you're questioning if that is sweat or pee on your chair.

Here are a few of my favourite gems that got me through the year. Hopefully there will be a good mix of jaw-droppers and pop-snorters.

- Holding up the urn as my cousins came to see me before the funeral at my grandparents' house, "Have you met my husband Quinn? He's looking a bit ashy these days."

- While joking to my aunts about dating, "I'll go on my first Tinder date wearing Quinn, my mom, and my dad's ashes on a necklace, then say to the man "Look, there's room for one more!"

- I kept joking to my friends I would spend the next year taking Quinn to all the places he'd never been in the world. You know, toss his urn off the Eiffel tower; throw it out of a plane while skydiving in New Zealand; submerge it while scuba diving the Great Barrier Reef. The possibilities are truly endless.

- A very good piece of advice from the females in my family: "The first marriage is for love, the second is often said to be for money; but actually, it's for good sex."

- After spending an hour with Quinn at his viewing, "I guess I'll never age. I've got enough formaldehyde on my lips to preserve these babies for life."

- Also at Quinn's viewing after I'd been alone with his body for about an hour, Quinn's sister looks at me and says, "Jeez, we all know you wanted a baby, but did you really have to try for one now?"

- When talking about dating, "Might as well start hitting up the retirement homes now. Quinn's life insurance won't last forever, so I might as well find me the next sure-thing. I think I could have 3 or 4 husbands in the bag by 30 if I play my cards right."

- Walking into a bar in downtown Calgary with my college bestie, Ashley, who also has had some unfortunate luck this year, "Is the cover-charge waved for a cancer patient and a worphan? We can't make this shit up, so we might as well milk it for all it's worth. "

- And probably the most controversial of all my jokes, when someone asked me where my husband was, I replied, "He seems to hang out in the garage a lot these days."

  #sorrynotsorry

Milestones

(February 2018)

Milestones are weird. You never know which ones are going to sting and which ones will pass almost without thought. It's like playing Russian roulette with dates on a calendar. Each big day, you pull the trigger, hold your breath, and pray you come out alive.

My beautiful and wonderful niece, Charlotte, was born just 6 days before her Uncle Quinn died by suicide. Six days before the world shattered and time stood still. Except it didn't. Time continued on without him. Charlotte grew. She grew, and she grew, and she grew. And don't get me wrong, I love, and will always love, watching her grow. I love every moment spent with her and every picture or video my sister sends of her. Charlotte, and my other nieces and nephews, truly are my little lights in this world of darkness that surround my soul on dark days. But every time Charlotte grows, every time she turns one month older, my heart breaks a little more. Because, as she grows older, Uncle Quinn's been dead longer. And he's missing out on every wonderful moment of her little life.

Ever since my parents' passing, my birthday has been extremely hard for me. June 6 used to be my all-time favourite day. My mom was a bit of an over-celebrator, as was I, and would decorate the entire house, buy way too many presents, and make multiple cakes for multiple birthday parties (you know the friend party, the family party, and the actual birthday party) to make sure each birthday was beyond special.

After she died, no one did that. Quinn's family didn't celebrate to the extent my family did, so my birthdays became quite a bit mellower with a tinge of sadness. It just no longer was the celebration it once was. And I began to resent birthdays, because birthdays simply reminded me of what was lost and what could never be found again.

The last birthday I celebrated with Quinn alive was a hard one for sure. Quinn's grandmother had passed away a few days before my birthday, and her funeral happened to be scheduled on my birthday. Unfortunately, I had a very busy schedule with work so had to stay home. And, honestly, I don't do well with funerals anymore and didn't particularly want to be at a funeral on my birthday. So, Quinn made the trip to Saskatchewan to grieve with his family and celebrate her life solo.

Since it was my birthday, Quinn had promised me he would go to the funeral and come home right after so he would be home for supper to celebrate my special day with me. Quinn's depression; however, hit him hard, and he decided to stay one more night with his parents. The hard part for me wasn't that he wouldn't be home on my birthday or that we wouldn't be having a celebratory birthday supper together, no, it was that all I received that day was one very short, to-the-point text. No phone call. No, "I'm sorry." No, "I'll make it up to you." Just a simple, "I'm too tired to drive home, so I'll see you tomorrow." Not even a "happy birthday, Babe." The grief took over and the depression consumed his brain, and my birthday no longer mattered to Quinn.

Please don't get me wrong, I truly understand how important it is to go home and grieve a loved one's death at a funeral, and I fully supported him going to his grandmother's funeral that day. What hurt me so much; however, was he had promised to spend the evening with me, which was unexpectedly broken. Quinn completely forgetting, or choosing not to remember in his state of depression, to wish me a happy birthday at all really just hurt. An already dreadful day was made significantly more excruciating and painful to work through without him here.

When Quinn came home the next day, he still did not wish me "happy birthday." He acted like everything was normal and nothing was wrong. He was actually mad at me for bringing up to him that he didn't wish me "happy birthday" and missed my big day completely. It took that stubborn husband of mine a solid three weeks of listening to me complaining and crying about my missed birthday without a cake, a card, or even a phone call, before he even acknowledged my birthday had passed. Eventually; however, he did clue in to my bitching, and he did try to make it up to me with cupcakes, flowers, a late birthday card, and finally, an apology.

The bright side of my forgotten birthday; however, was that we had moved to such a wonderful neighbourhood here in Cochrane. And, when my incredible neighbours heard I was going to be alone for my birthday, they came over, took me out for supper, and brought me over wine and cupcakes.

Quinn and I did celebrate many wonderful birthdays together before the last one. And, he always made a point to do something special for me on each and every other birthday we were together. He attempted to bake cakes, bought me flowers, and got me the gift he knew I wanted. And, almost always ruined the surprise by giving it to me weeks before my actual birthday, so he'd often end up getting me a second gift to open on the day of…which I never objected to.

But this was the LAST birthday I ever spent with my husband. The fucking last one. And it was horrible. What a memory to cherish the rest of my life. What a way to add to the already shitty day I call my birthday.

The hardest part for me; however, isn't that Quinn "ruined" my last birthday. No, what makes it so damn hard is that every time my birthday comes around again, I notoriously grow older.

Real light-bulb moment there, Zoe. Glad you know basic math.

I grow older with each birthday but Quinn doesn't. And he never will again. Quinn will never grow old with me. He will forever remain 25-years-old. That's it. That's all.

And, you know, I don't want to be older than him. He was always a month older than me and liked to rub that in my face any chance he got. My birthday now signifies me growing old without him. Quinn will never celebrate 26; or 27; or 30; or 40; Or the big 5-0. Never.

But I will. I will grow old *without* him, instead of *beside* him. And I don't want to know what it will feel like in 20 years to look at a picture of my Quinn and see him as a child. I don't want to know what it feels like to watch my own children turn 25 and think that my own damn children have now lived more life than the true love of my life. I just don't want to know.

But yet, it's inevitable. I will be that crazy old lady, wheeling around the old-folks' home at 85-years-old with my nighty on backwards and my hair out so far it looks like I've been electrocuted, with a picture of a 25-year-old gorgeous man in hand asking my friends if they've seen my husband, Quinn, because I need him to go change the oil on my SUV and pick up our dog on his way home. And every single day, someone will have to tell me he died 60 years ago. And the hurt will hit once again like a semi hitting a smart car.

Is This Real Life?

(May 2018)

"Is this the real life. Is this just fantasy?" –
Queen

Seriously, is anything real anymore? Or are
we just living in some sort of virtual reality
where some crazy Hitler-type is messing
with my head to see how much stress a
human brain can take before falling apart
entirely.

I mean truly, how else do you explain this
fucked up hand of cards I was dealt with?

I'm not going to start the God debate, but it
truly makes no sense how some all-powerful
being would just sit back, relax, and watch
Zoe's world blow to smithereens, then just as
soon as Zoe has picked up the pieces that
were salvageable enough to build again, he
dropped a nuclear bomb and refilled his
popcorn bucket.

I feel like even Virtual Reality has a bit more
merit than plausible explanation.

But really, sometimes even my thoughts
don't seem like real life anymore. Today, for
example, I actually had the thought pass

through my brain that I wished I had been an awful wife and cheated on Quinn, so that I would at least have had someone to hold me and rock me to sleep at night after he died.

Where do these thoughts come from? Hallucinogenics? Narcotics? My "casual" wine drinking?

Relax, dear sister. This is my twisted humour coming through. Don't feel you need to check me into the nearest rehab facility the moment you put this book down. I promise you all of this pure comic genius stems straight from my sober cerebrum. Well… most of it.

But really, those crazy thoughts I sometimes have stem from real worries, real fears, real experiences, and real emotions. And at some point, I'm going to have to pack up the rest of Quinn's stuff, put on my big girl panties, shave my legs, unplug the hair in the shower drain, and try to find love again.

Because, can I tell you a secret?

Being alone sucks. Like really sucks. Full-blown Kansas twister, sucks.

I used to enjoy nights when I got to be alone. I actually looked forward to nights when Quinn was working shifts so I could have a night to myself. I could lay in the bathtub far too long, with a glass of wine that was judgmentally large, and a far too trashy of show on Netflix to watch. Well, I've now had far too many of those alone nights. But the alone nights I've had lately haven't been the serene retreat I once looked forward to. Instead, they've been slashing reminders of the loneliness I've felt and the emptiness inside my home and my heart.

But sometimes, I feel the most lonely not when I'm sitting at home with my dog night after night, but actually when I'm surrounded by a group of people all sitting on their phones, texting or calling someone who loves them. Someone whose world would change horrendously if their loved one didn't walk through the door to their house that night. Someone who wouldn't know where to go or who to turn to if they were gone in a single instant. Someone whose heart would be shattered into a million little pieces that could never be picked up. Someone like me.

And, the part that hurts the most is there's no longer a person like that in the world who would feel that way if it was me. If it was me who never walked through that door. If it was me who was gone in a single instant. I no longer have a "person." I no longer have someone who would feel the gut-wrenching pain I felt when Quinn died. I'm nobody's somebody.

Yes, I'm very aware that I have a lot of people who love me. I was lucky enough to be born into a large and loving family, and somehow I managed to build very strong friendships around me during the last 25 years of my life. But it's just not the same. All of these people have mothers and fathers, husbands and wives, or children of their own. They all have someone they would lay down their lives for without thinking twice about it.

I'm not that someone.

I know I'm a very important someone in a lot of peoples' lives. I really do get that. But when push comes to shove, I'm not the one anyone needs. I'm not the one anyone craves. I'm not the one anyone thinks about first thing in the morning or last thing at night. I'm just not.

That is my reality. And that is a battle in itself I must overcome every day because, honestly, that's a pretty hard pill to swallow. And, on really hard days, days when I don't want to get up in the morning because the anxiety is weighing me down and making it hard to breathe, the thought of being nobody's somebody eats me alive.

Can I tell you a secret? Some days, when that anxiety creeps up and tries to eat me, I get a pretty scary thought. A thought that replays in my head, often getting stronger and stronger, until I feel it trying to take hold of me and consume me. I get the thought that, at some point, mental illness is going to take me too. That all of the advocacy I do to end the stigma and speak out about how ok it is to not be ok; all of the posts I share on social media; all of the suicide prevention walks; all of the podcasts I speak on; and all of the books I write may end up helping a lot of people, and I truly hope they do, but they won't end up helping me. Sometimes, I feel that all of my efforts will be for other people, and in the end, once I have told my story and feel my words have touched enough people, the same ending that took my husband is coming for me. Because, how do you actually recover from such a depth of trauma?

Still not suicidal, folks.

I don't think about ways to kill myself. I don't think about how everyone would be better without me. I don't think about how shitty my life is and how no one will notice if I'm gone. I don't have suicidal thoughts.

But sometimes, when I'm at my loneliest, I do have an intense feeling that somehow, someday, I'm going to finish my purpose here on earth and the only thing I'll want is to be in my Quinn's arms again, listening to some good ole fashioned Rock and Roll with my dad, and eating a rather large piece of my mom's famous pavlova by her side.

And, I'm honestly really looking forward to that day.

The Dating Life

(May & July 2018, January 2019)

One of the hardest realities about not having a husband anymore is the simple reality that I am now officially single again. Widowed, yes, but single. The last time I was single was in the year 2009. And giiiirrrrl let me tell you something; in that "short" amount of time the dating world has changed substantially.

Substantially. I mean, back when I was single the last time around you actually had to meet the person. In-person. Not online. Not on some app. Like actually physically grow some balls and ask a real-life person out in real life.

Crazy, right?

Seriously, what is this "online dating" thing? I mean, I grew up in the time of MSN Instant Messenger, when MySpace was so much cooler than Facebook. Now you can literally download an app (one of many), post a few pictures of yourself and a short bio of 50 words or less, then swipe right or left looking to find your next "Prince Charming." Or late night hook-up. Whatever floats your boat, no matter how weird you like your boat floated, you can find it online.

Testing the Waters

When is it actually "socially acceptable" to go on a date after your husband dies? Honestly, I'm not sure if there is a true answer to this question.

After about two months of being a widow, some of my closer friends were telling me I needed to get out there and "break that seal" to help me move on. Others, mostly family members, were telling me I needed at least a year alone to grieve and be ready to let someone in.

Who was right? Probably neither.

By the end of October, I needed something. What that something was, I'm not entirely sure now as I look back. But what I did know was I needed to feel something other than intense pain and sadness. So, I listened to my friends and joined an online dating app.

And it felt good to be wanted. To have men interested in me. Whether they actually wanted to get to know me, just liked what they saw, or were only interested in a "taste." In the state of grief I was in, I truly didn't care. It just felt good to feel something. So I

tested the waters and talked to a few guys.
And I met a few guys. And "broke that seal."
In a few different ways.

M

The first time I went on a real date was
simply terrifying. I had never met this guy in
person, we'll call him M, and I was so
worried he'd be a creep, a serial killer, or
something completely different than his
online persona.

But you know what? He wasn't any of those
things at all.

He was kind, and he was smart. He was
relatable and interesting, and he made me
laugh when I thought I couldn't. The first
night we went out, we talked for three hours
straight. And it felt really good to just chat
with someone new. M was a gentleman and
didn't try anything on the first date, but he
did ask for a second. And I said yes.

Our second date was simple; we took our
dogs to the dog park and just walked and
talked. Again, a great date. But, truth-be-
told, the timing just wasn't right. M was a
"perfect" guy. He was exactly what I needed;
just one year too early.

You see, at that point in my grief journey, I wasn't looking for anything long-term. I was looking to fill a need. Not a forever need. So finding someone so wonderful scared the living crap out of me. And I ran. Without giving him an explanation, I just ran.

Looking back, should I have ran? Probably not. M was a really great guy and genuinely seemed to care and want to be with me. In the months after running, I thought about him from time to time and wondered if I should have ran or not, but I don't regret my decision to end it. I was not ready for a long-term relationship at all, and I know that's what he wanted. I needed time to find myself and make one or two, or five, or eight mistakes first. But I shouldn't have just ran. I shouldn't have "ghosted" M like I did.

A slow ghost, yes, but a ghost none-the-less.

Ghosting seemed easy to me. I got rid of him fast and didn't have to explain myself. But what I didn't realize at the time was how painful ghosting is. How many unanswered questions it leaves a person with. I didn't realize how awful it feels to be on the receiving end of the ghost. And for that, I regret ghosting him. He was a good guy and in another life, we might have worked out pretty great. He never deserved to be left wondering why I left. No one really deserves that.

<u>T</u>

In May, after months of bars and booze, and being, frankly, a bit reckless, I finally met someone I actually stopped and thought twice about. We'll call him T. This someone, whom yes, I can admit I also met on some trashy dating app, actually seemed to get me and held my interest. I knew he was something special when he took the time to ask me what I thought my own best qualities were. He made me laugh and impressed the hell out of me when he would quote song lyrics and I got the reference each time. He played bass in a band and had the most random pet hedgehog with an equally random name.

He didn't ghost me the moment he learned about my challenging past. Instead, he told me it made me more likeable and that I was someone he wanted to get to know more of. He also shared with me how he got to where he was now, and talked openly about the shit he had also faced. Not my calibre of shit of course, but still shit for a normal person. He allowed himself to be vulnerable with me, and I actually let myself be a little bit vulnerable with him too.

He was funny, but not quite as witty as me, and he was handsome; like almost Quinn-hot. Although, I'm sure no one wants to hear about how they measure up to my dead husband on the hotness scale. But real-talk ladies, I was the solid letdown in that relationship when it came to looks.

So, I took a chance, put on my big-girl panties and my favourite red lipstick, and I met the guy.

In all honesty, I'm terrified of meeting new guys. Absolutely terrified. Especially new guys who seem pretty awesome. So, what did Zoe do to prepare for this meet?

Drink. And drink. And drink.

Was this a mistake, you may ask?

Well it wouldn't be such a fun story if it wasn't, right?

So anyways, fast-forward to a slightly intoxicated Zoe and her very good pal, Ashley, stumbling into some bar in downtown Calgary to watch T's band play and see if he was as great in-person as he was via text. By the way, if you every need a wingman, hit up Ashley. She gets to the point and gets things done. She marched straight over to that stage and yelled at T, "Zoe's here!!"

Holy sweet baby Jesus, I guess he knew I was there now.

After his set finished up, he came over and started chatting with us. He was genuine and sweet, and he actually seemed excited to meet me too, as he gave me a big hug and seemed genuinely interested in what I had to say. I truly believed we hit it off and was really excited to see where things might go. T had to load up his band equipment though, so he brought his buddy over to keep us company while he drove his equipment home.

And, this is where it started to go to hell.

You see, T's buddy, we'll call him B, was very nice to me. Very. And, real-talk again, I can be quite the flirt, as all witty women are. And that flirtiness has been known to grow with alcohol. That alcohol had definitely begun to set in by this point.

So B was keeping us company, and Ashley and I, as good old college roommates do, started making some hilarious, albeit sexual jokes towards each other. And, since we are such good friends and two very loud and open individuals, there's a good chance we're going to get all up in each other's business, which, apparently, guys dig.

Well B really seemed to enjoy that, and thought he would try to join in on our fun. But, that fun wasn't for him, and I made it pretty clear I wasn't interested in him and was solely interested in T.

Eventually, T came back and we talked some more. One thing led to another, and we started getting closer and closer, and he leaned in and kissed me.

Can I tell you a secret? It felt pretty good. It felt like that kiss could be the start of something really great. Maybe not long-term; most likely not forever; but something good for now. And I needed something good; something to look forward to; something new and easy, like a breath of fresh air.

It wasn't like the kisses I had been used to months before when I was at my lowest in the journey called Grief. The kisses without any emotion to just fill a space in an empty bed. This particular kiss had a bit of spark behind it, and he was sure to comment on my ridiculously large smile and blushing cheeks when we pulled up for air. Because, let's face it, kissing him made me happy. A feeling I wasn't particularly used to.

Fast forward to a few moments later when T had left the table to grab drinks and B came back. I was still a solid level of drunk when B came up to me and grabbed one of my boobs while laughing away. I remember looking at him, looking down at my boobs, and looking back up at him again before saying, "really dude?" and swatting his hand away.

Well, I never saw T again.

Apparently, T and B talked (or T saw B grab my boob) and decided I must be into B, so he walked out. He didn't wait to ask me what happened. He didn't care for my side of the story or to hear that his friend was in the wrong. He didn't want to realize his friend assaulted a girl he was getting to know and seemed genuinely interested in because, God forbid, you always have to believe your buddy is a good person over some girl you just met on an app. So, he left. And I was stuck sitting there confused as hell.

To make matters worse, once T had disappeared B came back, grabbed my boob a second time, and said, "So if you're not going to go home with T tonight, how about you at least give me a blowjob?"

Wow. What a winner there. I wish I had pick-up lines that were that great.

So, needless to say, we left the bar. Sans blowjob.

That night, I may have shed a tear or two. But, on the upside, no barf was hurled.

The next day, I convinced myself T left the bar for some important reason, and he would text me that reason that day. But, he never did. So, since I'm all about the open and honest communication, I texted him. Hours went by, and I thought it was a lost cause until finally, T did text me back. He told me how wonderful I was, and that I was smart, funny, gorgeous, and sassy, which were all qualities he was looking for in a girl, but that I seemed much more interested in B than him, so he just wanted to be friends with me. He never asked for my side of the story. Never thought to consider maybe B was jealous or just wanted to try to find an "easy" girl himself.

Or, maybe he really just wasn't into me. Maybe it finally hit him I was an orphan and a widow with baggage too heavy for him to carry. Maybe he got one look at my ass and realized I could open my own cell tower on it and decided he was much more into skinny girls. Who knows what he was really thinking. All I know is he ended it. Just like that. A solid case of the slow ghost technique, which I thought was my specialty.

And, honestly, I've never been friend-zoned before. I've never known what it feels like to actually start liking someone, be interested in their life and want to be a part of that life for however long it may last, then suddenly be ghosted by them.

Way back when I used to actually date guys, I never lost. Yes, I would have moments where I got rejected, but, if I waited long enough and played the game just right, I always came out with the guy. And in all honesty, the part that really got me with T was that he became disinterested in me because of something his friend said about me and not by the fact that I was a widow or an orphan. This truly is something I don't think I'll ever understand. Which is a real shame, because I honestly thought there could have been something pretty great between us.

E

Now E came out of nowhere, and I warned him from the start I'd break his heart. But E never listened to my wise advice, and I'm pretty sure I broke his heart, although I truly never meant to hurt him at all.

You see, when I ran into E at a wedding in… wait for it… Manitoba, I had finally stopped looking for men. I had already had my share of fun and frustrations and finally realized I wasn't ready to be looking for anyone. But, as fate would have it, into the church I walked for the rehearsal and my eyes fell straight on him; the only one I had yet to meet in a room full of country guys and gals. And, we all know how Zoe likes to flirt, so I just couldn't restrain myself.

E was a quiet guy, and I thought for sure my loud, outgoing, and strong personality would scare him right out of Manitoba. Only, somehow, it had the opposite effect entirely. Instead of running away, my crazy laugh drew him in. He laughed at my jokes, he listened with interest to my stories, and by the end of the night I just felt something click.

The next day, we hit it off again, and I felt myself getting silly butterflies from the rush of someone liking me back; a feeling quite foreign to me in recent days that beckoned me towards it, as if it was a drug I'd long since given up but craved dearly. I let myself get wrapped into it, and I let him get wrapped into it as well. With a mix of gin, wine, rum, and a pair of pyjamas locked away in a house, I woke up next to him, slightly resembling a tramp in a very small tent, in a very small town, still in my bridesmaid dress.

This was the first night I slept with a man that wasn't Quinn. And I mean truly in the "sleep" form, complete with lumberjack snoring, no doubt coming from my very drunk and sleep-deprived nose. And that was the scary part. I spent the whole night in another man's arms just *sleeping*. It was a first I made sure never happened all year. And, suddenly, there it was. And it felt good, which terrified me to my core. But, it also excited me and reminded me just how good falling asleep in someone's arms, someone who cares about you's arms, felt.

When I boarded my plane the next morning, I let him fall for me. And, to be honest, a piece of me tried to fall for him too.

For a little while, I thought maybe he could be the something good in my life I was searching for. So I stayed in contact with him even though I was flying halfway across the world the next day. And we talked, and we laughed; and it felt nice.

But suddenly, while I was snapping photos of temples in Thailand to send back to him, I had a realization: I liked being just Zoe. I liked being independent and flirty and free to do what (and whom) I wanted. I didn't want to be the girl constantly waiting for some boy to text her back, FaceTime her at night, or call her in the morning. I didn't want to be sending memories back to him when I should be living in every moment for myself. So, slowly and steadily, I distanced myself from him, and let him go completely.

I know he never quite understood why I left, and I honestly don't think he got over me as he tried to win me back with funny texts, photos, and even some gorgeous surprise flowers to brighten my day, but I just couldn't do it. I couldn't allow myself to be vulnerable and I couldn't allow myself to belong to someone. So, I did what I do best; I turned off my emotions and made sure to catch flights and never feels.

And, I started to look for my next conquest. But, what happens in Thailand, stays in Thailand...

But you, E, are nothing short of amazing. And, in a different life, maybe I could have chosen you. In this life; however, our stars didn't quite align. So keep searching, E, you're going to find the sun to your moon. And she's going to be one hell of a lucky girl. I just know it.

The Hunt for Perfection

(July 2018)

So, what exactly am I looking for in my next keeper? Well hey, boy, hey, do I have a list for you. And ladies, take note, you yourself should also sit down and make a list. If a man isn't meeting three or more of those qualities in your life, hunny, it's time to walk. You deserve to find the man you're looking for because, from what I've learned this year, there are PLENTY of other single men out there waiting to get to the front of your line. You *can* find Mr. Right. Don't settle for Mr. Sometimes Okay. I'm crossing my fingers that I too can find a second Mr. Right to keep me company at night and support me through each and every day.

I didn't find my next "Mr. Right" over the course of the last year, but what I did learn was exactly what I don't want in a man. I now know where *not* to look to find a keeper, because the free dating apps and 1:00am bar meet-ups, although lots of fun and quite exciting, are not exactly where stand-up men reside. Note to self, ladies, if you give a man a nickname with your girlfriends he is most definitely NOT the one. No, I'm not looking for a "Clay the Ginge" or a "Maybe Dylan," and I'm certainly not looking for a "Pierced Peter," "Toothless," or anyone with the initials B.S., as they are definitely full of bullshit and deserve nothing less than a big bag of anonymous dicks send to them on Valentine's Day. This of course being a "random," albeit hilarious and very satisfying, example of something one might do to someone who treated him or her like dirt. And, I'm definitely not looking for any "Married Morgans," because never do I ever intentionally want to add the title of "home-wrecker" to my list of accomplishments in life.

What I can take from this year of dipping my toes back into the dating pool is a list of qualities I now know I want and some very vivid reminders of what I definitely know to avoid next time. But what I do know now with the most certainty is I am worth what I am looking for.

Let me say that again so we can both let it sink in.

I am worth what I am looking for.

I am worth it. And I will make someone very happy again. But he will make me even more happy because he will be just right for me. I deserve to feel love and happiness once again. When I'm ready, I will find my next blue-moon love. And that blue-moon man will love me for me. He will love me for the woman I have become. He will love me for the battles I've fought. He will love me for my scars, my struggles, my dark and twisty edges, and for my mistakes. He won't want to change me, tame me, or make me anything I don't want to be. He will love me for me and that will be enough. One day, I will tear down the walls I've spent the last year building up around me, and he will see **me.**

Qualities I'm Looking for in a Man:

- This man better be genuine, straight-up, and honest. I like when a man calls a "spade a spade." This is something my daddy taught me was very important in a person, and he couldn't' have been more correct.
- Someone who treats me well and treats the janitor as well as he treats the principal.
- Someone who loves my dog, almost as much as I do.
- A man who is almost as funny as I am, because let's face it, this calibre of wit is somewhat hard to come by.
- Now for the shallow side of me....I like a man who's at least 5'9 and handsome as hell, with some killer ken hips. You know, ladies, the "V"

leading to the "D." A couple of tattoos never hurt anyone either.

- A man with maturity who has had some life experiences of his own that makes him experienced, humble, and wise.
- Someone who is easy going, loves to have fun, and isn't prone to jealousy.
- A true family man, who loves his family but is also his own person capable of making his own decisions, and also loves and respects my family in addition to his own.
- A man who will love me for me and not try to "fix" me. This man will have to be ok with my past and understand that Quinn will always be part of my story and a piece of me will always love Quinn, even when I love this new man. I want a man who doesn't feel threatened by the ghost of Quinn and is ok with me talking openly about my memories with and of Quinn.
- A man who knows his way around a garage and is handier than I am.
- I want a man who has stable mental health. I used to say if a man had a history of mental illness, I would walk; however, I've come to realize it's the untreated or unstable mental health that is the problem. If someone has struggled with their mental health, but has sought treatment and is open to

treatment when problems arise, then I would be open to testing those waters.

- My next man must be a non-smoker and will not be an alcoholic. I am 100% ok with someone who drinks, because GIRRRL, I'd be a hypocrite if I said I wasn't; however, I want a man who can drink and still be in control. If they change into someone else after a few drinks, I walk.
- My next man must see a relationship as two people on the same team and will always have his partner's back.
- He must be established with a stable job he is happy with and without significant debt. I don't want a man who is a "project."
- I would seriously love a man who knows how to cook and likes to take care of his lady.
- He must be adventurous and have a zest for life. I want someone I can see the world with and share in new adventures and experiences with.
- This man needs to make me a priority. I don't just want to be wanted when it fits into his schedule; I want to be valued and treated with respect. I want to be someone's first choice.
- Finally, I want a man who isn't afraid to show his love. Someone who will snuggle me at night, hold me when I

cry, and want to share me with the world.

So, Future Lover, are you up for the challenge?

Finding Home

*(July 2018- sitting at a small coffee shop in
Tring, England, eating a brownie and
enjoying a large glass of proscecco)*

Home is something I've been searching for
over a rather long period of time. It is
something I can often grasp but not hold
onto, and I have yet to find a way to keep it
as my own.

Home was once a place.

I grew up on an acreage north of Unity,
Saskatchewan, with my parents, sister, and
my border collie, Gyp. This place was home
for 22 years. I knew every corner of our 21-
acre yard, spent afternoons in the shop
working on tractors with my dad, and
picking berries and watering the ridiculously
large garden with my mom. I spent
countless hours imagining I was going on a
"dinosaur hunt" through the "woods" behind
our house to find fossils on the giant rock
that inhabited our front field. And by giant, I
mean giant; it was a good 2-foot jump to get
on it, and you could fit 6 children lying down
side-by-side on top of it. I also learned, in
later years, it was a great spot for Quinn and
I to go and have some "alone time," hidden
from the prying eyes of parents.

Then, just like that, home vanished. On September 10th, 2014, my father's depression took hold of him and, to put it simply, he just snapped. Now, this book is not meant to be about the death of my parents, so I'll keep it short. But what I can say about their deaths is they were never meant to be. It was not a "planned" act of violence. It was not an act that stemmed from years of physical abuse and violence from a murderous husband. It was a symptom of an untreated mental health disorder that unfortunately resulted in the worst manifestation imaginable. Or really I should say unimaginable, because in the 22 years I knew and loved my parents, never did I ever once think a tragedy anywhere near this horrendous would ever unfold.

My dad was eerily very similar to my husband, Quinn. It is often said that you marry your father, and I truly believe I did just that. I remember a few times when Quinn and I had started dating I'd come upstairs all pissed off that Quinn was an hour later than he said he'd come visit only to learn that Quinn came exactly when he said he would; he just came to visit my dad instead of me. The two of them would be seated upstairs chatting over a game of basketball, or they would be out in the shop looking under the hood of Quinn's car, completely forgetting about the entire reason they had become acquainted…ME. When the two of them were together, I was often the third wheel. Thanks, boys. Appreciate that.

Anyways, my dad truly was my best friend. He was an angel in a mechanic's body, who only showed his wings to select people. Which, I'm most certain, is why when he died the way he did, people spoke so horridly of him. My dad was a quiet, gentle soul, a lover of all things in nature, and a real rocker at heart. If there was a band Dad wanted to see, Dad would be there pumping his fist and singing along to every song, with his little rocker girl singing along right beside him.

But, my dad was also lonely. He owned and operated his own business, British Tractor Wreckers, and he lived over 6000kms away from his family in England. Yes, he had my mom, my sister, and me in Canada with him, but Sarah and I grew up and moved out, as children do. My mom, who was a very busy woman with a very big heart, spent most of her time helping others in the community and rarely got home before 7 or 8pm. And, if she did get home earlier, she'd go straight out to the garden or begin prepping for work the following morning. Yes, I know lonely doesn't give him an excuse to go and kill my mom, but it does give an insight into part of what led him to fall into the deep and very serious level of depression he did over that last summer of his life on earth.

My mom was, for lack of a better word, a saint in the community. She dedicated her life to helping others and was dead-set on making sure every other person in her world was happy and had their needs met before she even considered whether she herself was happy as well. She was a true giver and "bucket filler." And, she was the most selfless person I think I will ever know. My mom had a laugh that could be heard and recognized for miles around. When you heard it, you couldn't help but smile yourself; it was a true "feel good" laugh. Thankfully, that signature laugh was passed down to me. And, I'm damn proud to have a laugh like hers.

As parents, I truly couldn't have asked for a better set. Their worlds truly evolved around their girls, and they would have given the world to make sure we had a lifetime of happiness. I'll be the first to admit, they were a rather odd fit: their personalities were on opposite spectrums, as were their parenting styles. Mom always made sure we were well-fed, well-behaved, and well-travelled, and Dad made sure we had a hell of a lot of fun along the way, even if the fun wasn't something Mom thought we should experience. But, there was never a question of love in our house. And, I always felt safe, valued, and needed in my family. That place, that family, truly was home.

Until it wasn't anymore.

As mine and Quinn's relationship grew, he began to become part of my home, and on the day my parents passed, he replaced that home entirely. Home was no longer a place to me; it had now become a person. And, my God, did I feel at home with him beside me.

Quinn was not always outwardly affectionate. He didn't always want to snuggle or hold hands, and he wasn't always the best with words. I do recall him once telling me I looked "short and stout" in a new dress. To his defence, he thought "short and stout" meant "cute and little," and he truly was trying to compliment me. All I said back to him was if he ever told me I resembled that of a teapot again, he'd be getting rather acquainted with his hand for the rest of his life.

But, he was my home, and he always had a way of making me feel so loved, nourished, valued, and respected. And, can I tell you the truth? I'm not quite sure I'll ever find a home as good as the one I had in him again.

When Quinn left this world, for a second time, my home left too. And, so where was home now?

Part of my journey this year has been just that, searching for home. Sometimes I feel it getting near, but it's not one that sticks. It's not something that feels so wonderfully right that I can keep it in my thoughts and cling to it in my life. It always feels like those moments when I feel most at home have a due date, and although I can go back to the library of life and re-sign out those books of home, sooner or later, I'll have to return them again.

As I said earlier, my house is no longer my home. I still feel it is my place of living, and I'm happy living there for now, but it has lost its sense of permanence. I now know I won't live there forever. I now know that the moment I start feeling something serious about another person I won't be able to stay there. This house will never be home to a life with someone else. It was a home to a life with Quinn, and that's how it will forever stay.

No, home to me now comes when I'm with certain people or when I visit certain places. It's fleeting, but it is there when I search.

It's there when I'm sitting with my best friends laughing so hard I think I may pee over our morbid or overtly sexual jokes. It's there when I'm playing with my nieces and nephews, breathing in each moment deeply when they're coming in for a cuddle. It's there when I'm enjoying a bowl of Borscht with my Baba (Grandma for you non-Ukrainians) in Macklin, when it's just us two widows. And, it's there when I'm out with my aunts in Calgary trying out a new recommended lunch spot. It's even there when I fly the 6000kms to my family in England, whom I may only see once every couple of years, but every time I'm with them, I feel like it has been merely days since our last visit together.

Home is every moment I spent with my sister, as she's the last remaining piece of my everyday childhood life, and it's most definitely in every visit I make out to Quinn's parents' farm in Cactus Lake.

Can I be honest with you? Although, I don't know why I keep specifying my honestly as this book is nothing less than my most honest and deep thoughts and feelings. If it were anything less than honest, it'd be pure rubbish. Anyway, the part I'd like to be honest about is during the entire time Quinn was alive, I don't think I ever once considered the Fisher farm my home. I couldn't back then allow this place and these people to become my home because I was so completely and overwhelmingly terrified that if I allowed them to become home, to become "Mom" and "Dad" and my second family, I would be replacing my old home and my own parents. And, that might lead to forgetting my lost home and parents. I just couldn't bring myself to do that.

After Quinn died; however, my outlook completely changed. You see, now Quinn's family became the last remaining shred of the home I felt with him. They were the last piece left in that lost puzzle, and I needed to hold onto it with both hands. Forever I will be thankful that they too needed to cling to me as the last piece of their son's puzzle as well. I know I can never replace Quinn and will never be Quinn to them, but I am so incredibly thankful they've taken me in and showed me only the love a true family can show another soul. And, let me tell you, Mr. Future-Lover, if you don't win their approval when one day I bring you home, you'll have a rather long walk ahead of you back to the city.

With that, although I have many glimmers of home in my new life, I just haven't quite found one place or one person that simply sticks. So, my hunt for home will just have to go on.

Coming Up for Air

(July 2018, England on the train from London to Lancaster / January 2019)

Grief definitely comes in waves. Correction, it doesn't come in waves, it comes in tsunamis. The kind that could take out an island and all the lovely pineapples growing along with it.

In December, I truly thought the worst of the grief was over. The initial fog that left me so shattered and weakened that I could barely make it off the couch or get more than a bite or two of food in my mouth had passed. Ok, you caught me. The exception was chocolate, mini eggs to be precise. And red wine. Plenty of red wine.

Anyway, the fog passed and I could see more clearly. I had slightly more energy, and my memory was stronger than that of a goldfish again. I was still devastatingly sad and my jokes were still hauntingly morbid, but I was able to begin to start living a "normal" life. I went to work, I went out with friends, I bought food and even made an odd meal for myself, and I walked my dog. I was surviving and "getting on."

But in April that grief hit again with a vengeance, and it seriously tried to take me and my pineapples right out with it.

You see, although the entire first year is a challenging one, there are certain dates and times that are going to be so much rougher than others. Spring in particular is a rough time for me, as there are many anniversaries that fall one after another. This second wave of grief started with my Mom's birthday, March 31st. And, although I had survived three previous birthdays without my mom, this one was by far the hardest, as it was a milestone birthday of 60 years young. A milestone my momma bear will never reach. A milestone birthday we couldn't celebrate. A milestone birthday I was supposed to remember with Quinn at my side.

The wave began to form.

Then came Quinn's birthday, April 28th. The first birthday marked without him here. The first birthday in which he never got any older but my age continued to increase.

The wave got wider.

Next up, my own birthday, June 6th. A day, as I've spoken about before, that no longer has such a sweetness but has become more and more bitter as more and more loved ones leave. A day in which I officially became older than my husband. A day I had been dreading since the day he died, just over 9 months before this day.

The wave grew higher.

That wave grew, and grew, and grew. It grew wider and higher until it was almost consuming me. I tried to swim, I really did give it my all, but I kept getting more and more tired the longer I swam. And I honestly didn't know if I could swim much longer.

And, I got scared. August was approaching, the one year anniversary of Quinn's death, and I truly didn't know if I'd make it until then. Although I was "getting on;" you know, going to work, getting groceries and cooking slightly more meals for myself, cracking jokes that were slightly less morbid, and indulging in less of a liquid diet and more of one with plants and proteins; on the inside I felt myself collapsing. It took almost every ounce of my energy to put on that brave face and make the world think I was doing ok.

Yes, I had a lot of good days. Days where I didn't cry, had belly laughs, and made some pretty wonderful memories. But, I also had really bad days. Those where I didn't really want to get out of bed because the mere thought of stepping into another day in a world without Quinn made me tremble, and if I found one more reminder of what I had lost, I might snap completely. On those days, somehow I got out of bed (no doubt because my beautiful and radiant dog, Layla, licked me until I smiled and pushed her off, so that I could heave my way out of bed to take her for her morning pee), drug myself into the shower, and put on my "war paint" to brave another day alone. In case you didn't have a dad quite as clever as mine, "war paint" was a term he often used to describe mine and my sister's makeup. Which, I think is a particularly accurate term to describe it now, as putting on makeup makes me feel fierce. If there's makeup on my face it conceals the fatigue and sadness I feel inside and makes it much more difficult to allow myself to shed a tear for fear of wrecking my freshly-drawn face.

The only way I got through it was to set goals for myself via dates that I couldn't allow myself to miss.

"If I can just make it until the end of April, I'll get to visit Auntie Jackie."

"If I make it to June, Sarah and Charlotte come."

"Just hold on a few more weeks, Zoe, then you get to see your nieces and nephew."

"One more week and you'll be safe again with your bridesmen and best friend."

"Breathe Zoe, you can make it to July and then you'll be in England."

Just make it to July, Zoe.

In truth, I just wanted out. And I didn't care how I got out. I just needed to be out of my life. Out of my house. Out of my town. Out of my world.

Fast. Out. Now.

And, I got out. I boarded the plane, and I breathed a deep sigh of relief.

And, slowly, the wave began to diminish as the Summer of Zoe commenced.

A Brief Introduction to the Summer of Zoe

(January 2019)

So what exactly was the "Summer of Zoe"?

It was the greatest gift I could give to myself; the largest form of self-care I could muster up to get out of my grief-laden reality.

It was a breath of fresh air; a stepping out of my life and letting go of all responsibilities to just focus on finding myself once more.

To do this, I knew I needed two things:
1) Something Old
2) Something New

And, since I wasn't planning on getting married a second time just yet, I skipped the "something borrowed and something blue," and jumped right into the Summer of Zoe with both feet. Because at this point, what the hell did I have to lose?

Something Old: Parkinson Family Time in the UK

(July 2017 / January 2019)

England has always been such a happy place for me. It's the one untouched piece left from my home.

Yes, I've had a few hard days in England: watching my sick grandparents die, attending my granddad's funeral, and having a second funeral and burial for my mother and father in England. But, the majority of my time spent in England has always been nothing short of wonderful.

My dad was an only child, but that didn't mean he didn't have a family. His family consisted of not only my late granddad and grandma, but also of my great aunts and uncles, cousins, and second cousins. And, just so we're clear, aunts and uncles don't have to be just the people who were born to the same man and woman who birthed your own parents. No, they are the people who love and nourish you as you grow from a child into an adult. The people who you can share a good laugh with or who will hold you a little bit tighter when you just need a good cry. They are the people you can confide in when you're not so sure what your mom or dad might say or do, and you know when you make all your dreams come true or fall straight onto your ass, they're going to be the first ones ready to congratulate you or peel you off the sidewalk. This is what aunts and uncles truly are, and I am bloody thankful to have so many in my court, in multiple countries.

So, although my dad was an only child, he had one hell of a wonderful family left in England and every single time we hopped across the pond to visit them we knew we'd be welcomed with open arms and so much love.

This particular visit was exactly that, and wow, did I feel the love.

This was the first time I had ever travelled outside of Canada alone (apart from living in North Dakota for six years of course). This was the first time I stepped on a plane by myself and woke up in another country.

Yes, I'm aware that when I got to my destination I was no longer "travelling alone," but you have no idea how scary taking those steps was. How scary it was to drop off my dog at her incredible sitter's house in Saskatchewan and fly 7000 kilometers away from her and every other comfort in my messy life.

But I knew I needed to go, and I knew I needed to heal. I knew I wasn't going to heal staying in a house that was once a home all summer long. I knew I needed to find that closure across the sea. I knew that to get closure myself I also had to give it to my Parkinson family, as I knew they needed to see me too to find their own closure and pass through the next steps of their own grieving process for Quinn.

Quinn only met my Parkinson family a few times. The first time he met the whole clan was my parents' English funeral. They were so warm and welcoming to him, and he instantly fell in love. And, although Quinn had a very hard time stepping on the plane and was incredibly overwhelmed by the busy airports and hustle and bustle of people, it was he who suggested we visit the Parkinson family a second time on our honeymoon.

I think Quinn found closure in my parents' deaths by being with the Parkinson family, as Quinn had such a special relationship with my dad. Just as I find my dad in them, Quinn did as well. So, in so many ways, me travelling to England after Quinn's death not only brought closure to me but also closure to them. They needed to see me. They needed to know whether I was ok or not ok. They just wanted to physically be there to

help support me through the grieving
process, and I so needed them to do that.

I was scared to get on the plane, but I was
even more terrified to get off it.

Why? Because I was terrified I wouldn't be
able to handle the stage of grief they were at
in my own stage of grief. I didn't want to
start that grieving process over, as I knew
their grief journeys were further behind than
mine. They weren't dealing with the grief
head-on each day; the ocean acted as a buffer
to that grief. Grief isn't quite as real when
that reality can't be physically experienced.
Their grief journey started when Quinn died,
yes, but it was put on hold for many months
until my sister visited them with her family
for Easter. Yet, even then the grief was still
in a slow zone, as the centre of that grief,
myself, hadn't graced their presence yet.

I was *terrified* to break that glass wall. I was
sure there would be too many tears, and I
didn't know if I could handle three weeks of
consoling others or falling back into an
earlier stage of grief that I had no desire to
go back to.

What if everyone was awkward around me
and tiptoed so quietly around the "Q" word
that we never even brought him up at all?

What if, worse yet, no one shed a tear?

What if no one in England cared that Quinn died? What would happen then?

Thankfully, going to England was exactly what my heart was craving. It was exactly what my heart needed to move to the next level of healing. When I got off that plane, there was nothing less than Parkinson family love. I was greeted with warm hugs, beautiful words, witty jokes, and, of course, plenty of bubbles and gin. Yes, there were some tears, but not the kind I dreaded. These tears were the kind that hurt but also healed.

In England during this journey of healing, I found I could be myself completely, w*ith no judgment.* I didn't have to put on a brave face at all. I didn't have to pretend I had a "normal" year. I didn't have to pretend I didn't have really awful days, make questionable decisions, and indulge in too many bad habits. I could laugh. I could cry. I could sink into their hugs. I could enjoy that fourth, fifth, or six drink without any disapproving eyes.

And I felt at home. I felt peace. I felt strength. I felt acceptance. I felt I was part of a family, a feeling I haven't been too familiar with in recent years. I felt like I belonged, and I so craved that feeling. Not distance, nor time, nor even degree of family relation changed that feeling, and I am so thankful for that.

England gives me such comforts: that sense of belonging, that feeling of home. From Bonds Farm on Duck Street to Liscoe Farm on Bodkin Lane, Tarnacre to Devil's Bridge, Garstang to Great Eccleston, Out Rawcliffe Village Hall and straight down to the bowling green, it all screams home to me.

This plot of grass is the most important spot in the entire world to me. This spot right here is where I'd choose to go over and over and over again if I was given the choice to go any place on earth. When I went to England this time around, this was the one place I craved to go. I needed to return to this one spot to hurt and to heal.

You see, even though this spot brings me
such heartbreakingly raw and piercingly
painful emotion, it also gives me peace,
tranquility, and calmness. This plot of grass
radiates the love that was shared by those
buried under this beautiful stone: my
granddad, my great aunt, my dad, and my
mom. The swords of my parents' deaths
were laid down and put to rest so that only
love remains in this one spot. To stand in a
space where my dad can be honoured,
remembered, and loved along with my mom
means more than you'll ever know.

Because, in Canada, this place does not exist.
In Canada, I was told he should be buried in
a ditch, as murderers and those who take
their lives by suicide should be. In Canada, I
was robbed of a safe place to go and grieve
both my parents; to take my wedding dress
to "show my daddy" before marrying the
man he loved like a son; to lay on my
daddy's grave as I cried over that same dead
love. I was robbed for a crime I didn't
commit because grief takes hold of people in
different ways, one of which is anger. An
anger that became misdirected at me for
some time, as I became the closest stand-in
to my father in the eyes of some grieving my
mother's tragic end. In many ways, I paid the
price for my father's crime, and it stung like
a sting I have never felt before.

But this spot here, in beautiful Lancashire, has only happy memories tied to it, and it so beautifully radiates the love my parents gave to me everyday. So when I returned this time, it was only fitting to bring a little bit of Quinn with me to this beautiful spot of love. And, it gave me great peace to know all my angels were at peace in that one beautiful place of love.

I so needed that peace.

Not only did I find closure in Quinn's death when I ventured back to England, but I also found some closure I didn't know I needed in the death of my dad. In Canada, no one really talks about my dad. He's kind of a "forbidden" topic to many people, as I think they feel like if they say something kind about my dad they are disrespecting my mom's memory. In England; however, my dad was family, biological family. He was also their friend and was loved without judgment. They knew my dad better than anyone else on the planet because they grew up with him, made mistakes with him, got into all kinds of mischief with him, and supported him through stages of his life long before my mom even entered the picture.

So, you have no idea what a breath of fresh air it was to hear people talk openly about him, to tell his stories (stories that would otherwise be lost forever) and to share all the things they loved about him with me. It was also incredible to just learn about my Parkinson family; my grandparents, my granddad's brothers and sisters, and my great grandparents. To hear about the Parkinson family history and the values our family has passed down to each generation. To learn where I got my quirks, where my sarcastic humour stems from, and how I got my thick ankles and crooked smile.

I felt *proud* to be a Parkinson again. "Parkinson," a name I didn't have to feel shame to bear in England. A name I could say with confidence and pride because it's associated in England, not with a sorrowful tragedy, but with a group of incredible human beings who value family, laughter, and love so highly.

"Honourably bold," a Parkinson family motto. We Parkinsons, I learned on this trip, "persevere and conquer." I now understood where my perseverance came from. Why I haven't given up and why I haven't stopped on my quest to conquer the world. I am a Parkinson, through and through. *A very proud Parkinson,* and I will live life "to the buckle end," as Parkinsons do.

What a beautiful gift it is to be a Parkinson. And, what a beautiful gift it was to return to

England and find that peace, assurance, and love I needed so badly during the "Summer of Zoe."

Something New: Life Lessons Learned in Thailand

(August 2018)

The second half of the Summer of Zoe was spent in Thailand. Now, if you've never been to Thailand, I have three words for you, GIRRRRRRLLLLLL go now. Seriously, before going to Thailand I had heard lots of amazing stories about how beautiful it was, how interesting the culture was, and how great the food was, but nothing prepared me for just how absolutely incredible Thailand actually could be. I mean of all the places I have ever travelled to, Thailand without a doubt, tops that list at number one.

There's something serene and almost magical about Thailand. A true beauty can be found everywhere you look and there really is a calming, stress-free, everything-is-going-to-be-ok vibe that radiates through the countryside. Even in the busiest of cities, you feel an inner peace and stillness that just can't really be described properly without experiencing it for yourself.

When in Canada, I really find myself feeling like an old lady. Like, actual widow-old. Almost like my body hasn't got the message that I'm a YOUNG widow, not an 85-year-

old grandma who can barely make it up a set
·of stairs. I so wish my body would get that
memo so I could feel high school-hot again.
To quote Steven Tyler, "dream on," girl.

Anyway, in Canada, my back hurts, my feet
hurt, my head aches, my stomach pains, and
I often feel bloated and tired. In Thailand;
however, none of those ailments bothered
me. I don't know exactly what it was that
appeared to cure all my ailments, but I really
felt better than I had ever felt in years. *Years.*
Maybe it was the hot, humid air or perhaps
the wheat-free, dairy-free diet that helped.
Living on "Thai Time" was also an asset, as
no one was ever in a rush to do anything or
be anywhere; we always got to where we
wanted or needed to go but there was never
any stress involved in getting there.

Whatever it was, I truly felt happy, whole,
nourished, and myself. And it felt fucking
marvellous.

There's something also to be said about
travelling with a group of people you've
never met before who come from a variety of
countries, cultures, and economical
backgrounds. I travelled to Thailand with my
cousin, Cameron. Side-note: This guy right
here is someone I cannot sing higher praises
about. He is my person and I truly don't
know how I would have survived this year

without this kid, and a lot of my Hewko family as well. There may not be a chapter dedicated to the Hewko love I got this year, but trust me; it meant the world to me to have my mom's family in my court as well. And yes, Cam, I will still call you kid when we are raising havoc in adjoining nursing homes sharing stories about lady boys and jaeger with the orderlies. Oh, and by the way ladies, this guy is single. And you'd be stupid not to hit him up. So send me a message, and I'll send you his digits.

See that Cammy, I can be a good wingman too. ;)

Anyway, back to Thailand…

I travelled with my cousin, Cameron, and in our 25-day journey through Thailand and Tokyo, we were lucky enough to share this time with three sets of fellow travellers. Each group had a slightly different dynamic, but each dynamic was wonderful and exactly what we needed at that moment during our adventure. I can honestly say that 98% of the life lessons I learned in Thailand were courtesy of the incredible people we met along our journey. And, to quote my favourite musical, Wicked, "Because I knew you, I have been changed for good."

So here we go, let's kick it off with some Life Lessons Learned in Thailand. And travelling friends, I did warn you; what happens in Thailand, goes in Zoe's book… But don't worry, I'll go easy on you all. The PG-13 version of events will have to suffice.

For now…

1. Never trust a first impression. People will always surprise you, often for the best.

   This is a statement I have never found to be more accurate before going on this trip. When you meet a new group of travellers, the first thing you do is put on your "Judge Judy" robe and try to figure out each member of the group. This was definitely a game Cam and I liked to play on our travels. "Solid Sheldon Cooper right there." "First. Vacay. Ever." "Shit, this guy is trouble." "Looks like we've found ourselves a cougar."

   Now, we weren't always so inaccurate about our predictions. But, more often than not, the initial impression we had about one of our fellow travellers proved to be very wrong. And it was almost comical to go back in our memories to the day we met them and realize the people we thought we had met in that moment were never people on our trip at all. The high-maintenance teacher being shamed for a muddy towel turned out to be an artsy, adventurous foodie with a heart of gold who loved to dance and would try anything at least once. The young and naïve party boy transformed into an old soul with a lot more life experience than you'd guess and related to me on much deeper level than I ever expected as he was just trying to find his own way and purpose in the world too. The well-travelled thirty-some-year-old who portrayed confidence and a near arrogance morphed into a lost soul still searching for himself and to find a truth and deeper meaning behind events leading up to his sudden desires to pack up his life and travel the world.

One by one, the masks came off and the souls beneath them were revealed.

Those souls were so much more beautiful than any of the masks that lay at their feet.

2. Age is merely a number.

I have been told many times by many people that I am an old soul. In my 26 years on this earth, I have lived through some pretty hard-core shit. So in many ways, I became old before I had a chance to be young. I grew up very fast when my parents died and grew old at a rapid rate after Quinn left. I still remember going to work on my birthday (the first birthday I celebrated at this place of employment) when one of my co-workers came up to me and wished me, "Happy birthday!" She then asked, very innocently, "What is this, your third 30th birthday?" It was my 25th birthday. I guess the title of "orphan" really added to those frown lines.

On this trip; however, I truly learned the silliness of judging people based on their age. Age doesn't amount to experience. It doesn't factor in hardships, stressors, education, goals, or dreams. It is simply just a number defined by a day on a calendar. And the age you feel really depends on your environment.

According to my birthdate I am 26. At home, I can honesty say most days I feel I'm in my mid to late thirties. Part of me wants to be young, wild, and free; I want to go out on weekends and get a little bit crazy, make a few mistakes and add a few more "I can't make this shit up" stories to my book. But, the other part of me, the sad, grief-stricken, worphan, feels like I could easily be approaching 70.

In Thailand, I really felt different. I felt an excitement for life again. A spark I didn't know I had left in me that morphed into a fire in which the flames couldn't be contained. I felt renewed. And free. And so very wild in the best of ways. You know, the skinny dip in the ocean with 8 of your new-found friends, kind of way.

I felt 21 again. And not the 21 that I was when I was actually 21. The past 21-year-old Zoe was a tied-down housewife-in-training finishing up her last semester of undergrad and waiting on acceptance letters to grad schools. She was real fun (insert eye-roll here.). But, in all fairness, she was exactly who I wanted to be at that point in my life. And I would've kept being her for the rest of my life, because I was incredibly content being that person with my Quinn.

No, this Thai 21 was exactly what 21 should be; carefree. With plenty of energy to stay up all night drinking, dancing, talking, swimming, and I'll end that list right there, as I did say this would be the PG-13 recount of events in Thailand.

But, I really did feel so much younger in Thailand. And although I liked to joke to my actual 21-year-old Londoner travelling friend that I was SO MUCH OLDER than him, he definitely kept me in check with a solid "Shuuuut up Zoe, you're NOT old," and to make me feel a little bit younger I'm sure, he'd add a solid "love" on the end of that phrase. And immediately, I'd reverse-age back to 21.

So remember ladies, you're never too old for a good beach party, houseboat party, or restaurant party, and even when you're 26, you can still, albeit slowly and painfully, learn how to "Floss" like the kids.

3. Stepping out of your comfort zone can lead you to beautiful realizations of who you were meant to be.

To be frank, I was scared out of my knickers to go across the world and live out of a backpack for a month in a foreign, non-English speaking country. Yes, I have travelled many times before. I've been to England more times than I can count on my hands, touring France and Scotland in the mix while there. I've gone on multiple hot holidays including Mexico, the Dominican Republic, and Tenerife, Spain, and I've toured most of Canada and plenty of the United States over the course of my 26 years. But never have I truly "travelled."

So what exactly is the difference between travelling and going on holiday? A group of us had this conversation on our trip, and believe it or not, there is a significant difference.

When you go on holiday, you go to sit on a beach with a drink in your hand, enjoying the luxuries of towel service, elaborate meals, and fancy excursions. This is the type of trip we all like to do to get away from our regular life and "live a little." I love going on holiday and enjoyed a few hot holidays this past year and in years prior.

Going on holiday; however, doesn't make you a traveller or a well-travelled individual. You don't experience the culture, the food, the night-life, and the atmosphere as you do when you're *travelling*.

So what's the difference?

Travelling is heading to a destination outside of the regular tourist district. It's enjoying the simplicity of living out of a backpack, carrying only the essentials with minimal clothes and toiletries (leave your hair straightener at home, ladies), and experiencing the local life in the most authentic way you as a traveller can. Eating street food; Staying in local homes and engaging in local dance, art, cooking, and traditions; Trying out local forms of transportation and viewing local heritage sights and historical monuments.

I had never actually travelled before I travelled in Thailand. But stepping out of that comfort zone was truly life changing for me. Living a simple life and experiencing everything first-hand was exactly what I was craving without even knowing that was what I craved. I found through the travels and new adventures and experiences, including playing with elephants and eating live shrimp (nothing tastes quite as good as something squirming in your mouth… or quite as bad actually), I was finding myself and embracing exactly who I was as an individual. I was falling in love with who that authentic person was. And, it felt so good.

And, let me tell you, I have without a doubt caught that legendary travel bug.

And, I'm very proud to say, that was the only thing I caught and took home with me while I was in Thailand.

4. Never be ashamed to show your true and honest self.

   You are the exact person you should be. Never alter that person because you think someone might not like you, think you're cool, or want to be your friend. There are always other people out there who do want to love and be around the *you* that is *you.*

There is something so freeing about letting all your guards down, getting rid of all your fucks given, and just being you. In Thailand, I made a deal with myself, to do just that. To be just me. Unfiltered. Unrated. Zoe. And I couldn't have been happier.

And people responded really well to unfiltered, unrated Zoe. And it truly was eye opening. I didn't have to pretend to be anything I wasn't to please anyone. People genuinely liked me for me, which was the best confidence booster I could have ever asked for. I was comfortable and confident in my own skin and that confidence radiated out of me so much that it started to rub off on others around me. That self-love and self-confidence that I was demonstrating began to seep into others in the group and they too began to be their own authentic, unfiltered, unrated selves. And, it was magical meeting and getting to know each individual person. Just as they were. No judgments, no hesitations, no masks.

Pure, unrated, beautiful, unique souls.

5. Laugh loudly and often.

I'm sure I've said it before, but the best piece of advice my dad every gave me was "if you don't laugh, you go crazy." And the best gift my momma ever gave me was my laugh. My wild, crazy, ridiculously loud, contagious laugh.

And, boy, did I laugh loud and hard in Thailand.

From peeing straight on the tracks in a squat toilet while riding an overnight train to Chaing Mai to opium museums with children playing under a table of phallic souvenirs, there were many times on our Asian Adventure I truly thought I was going to wet my pants. And if I had, that probably would've just made us laugh harder and longer. Because once you get Zoe started on the giggle bus, you're going to have to make a lot of stops before she gets back off of it.

6. Take a hug when offered.

A very short and sweet life lesson. If someone offers to give you a hug, embrace it and embrace them. You can never have too many hugs, except, of course, when there is a line of huggers bursting outside the church at a funeral to hug you until your ribs bruise and your makeup is on 1000 different shirt collars.

So hug hard, hug a bit too long, and let that love radiate from your soul to theirs.

7. Experience every moment you're living in. They will only happen once.

At the beginning of the trip, as you all already know, I spent a bit of time sending my memories back to a certain E I had met just before jetting off to Asia. More like a lot of time, as I was caught up in the thrill of someone interested in me, so I spent too much time sending pictures to him, texting him, and Face-Timing him almost every morning. However, just over a week into my trip, I came to my senses after a sort of "British

Invasion" and realized I LOVED being fierce and independent, I loved being a free and flirty bird, and I loved and craved living in every single moment. So that's what I did. I started living. I started taking in every sight, scent, touch, and taste, and creating a hotbox of vacation euphoria to breathe in and get high off of.

And, high I was.

Ok family, chill: strictly high on life.

The only Thai drug anyone took on our trip was from a pharmacy, which is another story that involved quite a lot of vomit... but let's save that story for another day.

Anyway, once I stopped to smell the flowers and take it all in, I started to really and truly find myself. Really and truly get to know what Zoe liked, wanted, needed, and loved. And I started to love myself too. You see, by valuing the little things around me and finding beauty in every moment of the life I was creating, I began to value and find beauty in my own life again. And I began to realize life was still worth living.

8. Sometimes it's ok to be selfish.
   Catch flights, not feels.

   Being selfish is often necessary, as
   you can't love and care for someone
   else unless you love and care for
   yourself first. And sometimes, this
   self-care and self-preservation comes
   at the cost of another soul's feelings.

   Never did I ever mean to hurt anyone
   this past year. This past year was a
   year of finding myself and part of
   that finding myself was meeting new
   guys and learning what dating or
   friends-with-benefits really was
   again. This exploration in the form of
   men helped me rediscover who I was
   as a person and also what I wanted in
   a future relationship. There were
   many great qualities in the guys that
   entered my life throughout the year,
   but none of them fit the mould I was
   re-creating for myself. None of them
   were just right. And, I wasn't ready
   to settle and lose the self I had so
   long searched for to a mediocre man.

   So, in every one of those
   "relationships," I fled. I ghosted (or
   slow-ghosted). I walked. I ran. I
   caught flights the moment they
   caught feels. Because, I wasn't ready

to catch feels, and so I felt nothing for these men. I know that in this process I broke some hearts, truly without meaning to. But, this is where the honesty comes into play again…

Ready for it?

I don't regret breaking any hearts this year. I don't regret having some fun and experimenting with what I want and need. I don't regret catching flights instead of feels.

That's what I needed, and I'm ok with needing that. I'm ok with being selfish right now. My happiness is more important to me right now, and that's ok.

9. It's empowering to be a feminist.

I didn't realize I was a feminist until recently when I was out for a walk with my dog, thinking about the past year and all the feelings and experiences it has brought with it. When I was in Thailand, my fortune was read by one of our absolutely incredible tour guides. While telling my fortune, he told me I had a very strong foundation of women behind

me, among other things. I laughed
the whole reading off and went about
having the time of my life on the
tour, not really thinking much about
the reading.

But suddenly on the walk with my
little Layla, it really hit me. I am a
product of countless strong,
powerful, fierce, resilient,
independent, and loving women
holding me up.

Yes, I have had many incredible,
inspirational men in my life. My dad;
my husband; my granddad; my
dyido; my father-in-law; my best
friends; and my brother-in-laws, to a
name a few. But in recent years, I've
got to experience the true meaning of
sisterhood. The true meaning of
women helping women. Women
supporting women. Women lifting
other women up. Women looking out
for other women. Women not
judging other women for their
fearless, individual journeys. And
that's pretty spectacular.

Every time I've fallen, and there's
been many, many missteps this year,
my tribe of fierce warriors have
picked me up with loving arms and

put me back on my feet. Women from my past that I hadn't spoken to in ages or women I just met and barely knew all stepped up to the plate and offered me their love and support without any expectations or riders. And I've never been so grateful.

So, women, continue supporting women. Continue loving other women and showing them care and respect. Let's not judge other women based on shoes we haven't ourselves walked in. Let's not gossip or bitch about the actions of another woman when we don't know their full story behind those choices they are making. I'm guilty too. Let's empower and uplift. Let's listen and learn. Let's create a generation of fierce and unstoppable women.

I am fierce. And so are you. I'm telling you this now, but ladies, no one really needs to tell you that but *you*.

You've got this.

So thank you, Jack, for reading my fortune and helping me come to this beautiful realization.

10. Your story matters. Share it openly and proudly. You can change the world.

While sitting in the Tokyo airport, as the Summer of Zoe was approaching it's end, I realized this was my final life lesson learned in Thailand. And this was the biggest lesson and the most important one I learned during the month.

Your story matters.

My story matters. Quinn's story matters. My parents' stories matter. They all matter. And, sharing it can, and *will,* make a difference.

During our month in Thailand, Cam and I ran into a lot of incredible people, and since we are both very open and bubbly people, I found myself sharing my story many times. And each time I shared it, I felt more powerful, more at peace, more humble, and more fierce.

My story is a shitty one; that I know for sure. Depression murdered my mom, destroyed my dad, and killed my husband, but it's not going to take me. Despite all the bad in my world, I'm still fighting, and I really, strongly feel it is my cross to carry to share this story with the world. If I can save one soul sharing it, I'm doing my part.

It was an incredible experience sharing my story over and over while in Thailand with fellow travellers. Telling my story prompted others to also open up about their own stories, their past or current struggles, and their personal battles with mental illness. What was truly amazing was after I had shared my story, those I had shared it with began flooding me with kind words and messages letting me know that their perspectives on mental illness, grief, and even life itself had changed after speaking with me. And that felt really damn good. It made me feel like what I'm doing in choosing to share my story with the world in a very open, honest, and raw way is making a difference.

My goal has always been to save just one life by telling my story. To change the fate of *just one soul*. If I can save just one soul, I can sleep at night knowing Quinn's life had meaning. My parents lives had meaning. Their stories are their legacies. And it is important we continue sharing their stories to open up the conversation about mental health. Open communication is key to understanding mental health. It is key to healing. It is key to making changes to make our society a society in which mental health is just as important as physical health. It really is ok to not be ok; some days you're not going to be fierce, and that is life. Take that day as a self-care day, or that week, or that month, and come back with a fire inside you. Because *you matter*. And we're going to change the world.

I will keep preaching, so look out world. Quinn's story isn't over and neither is mine.

This year, I've learned I'm fierce enough to move my own damn mountains. And I'm not quitting anytime soon.

One Year, and It's All Beige

(September/October 2018)

That's a wrap, boys. August 31st has come and gone.

I did it.

I survived an entire year without my rock.

Entering into the one-year mark, I was terrified. I didn't know how I would feel when August 31st rolled around. Would I break down in an unending flood of tears? Would I not be able to get out of bed and fade into another deep and dark month of depression? Would my witty jokes get substantially wittier? Or worse yet, would my jokes stop being funny at all?

Truth is, I felt none of the feelings I thought I'd feel. I felt beige. Flat. Emotionless. Stoic.

Beige.

Exhausted, and beige.

You see, the tiredness you feel when someone who penetrates every piece of your soul dies is a tiredness I truly believe few understand. And I truly hope only few ever acquire an understanding of it. It's a fatigue that sleep doesn't fix. It's an exhaustion that caffeine won't damper. It's a whole body and mind collapse that you just can't shake. Because every single piece of you is completely and utterly knackered just trying to muster up the strength to exist. Your body becomes so drained and empty that you no longer feel pain, you no longer feel sadness, you no longer feel basic body functions like the need to pee or hunger. You just no longer feel. You truly even lose the ability to think, and your memory becomes that of a goldfish; 5 seconds pass, and it's all gone.

So, how did I survive this first year?

I'm not 100% sure.

The first few months were spent in a trance. I can remember bits and pieces of those days, as I said before, but a thick veil of fog clouds the memories that arise. The first few months I did not live; I just survived. And if it wasn't for the help of my friends and family who were constantly by my side, feeding me, and cuddling me for countless hours on the couch to try to get me a few hours of sleep each day, I would not have survived those first few darks months.

The next few months, we'll call the "Reality Months," where I basically lived as if I were playing a lead role in a reckless reality show. Those months were also cloudy, but with a haze of smoke from partying, drinking, and doing everything I could to numb the raw pain of loneliness that had finally started to seep into my conscience.

It wasn't until well past the six month marker of my first year of widowhood when I started to heal, although extremely slowly with a "two steps ahead, and a large glass (or bottle) of wine back" momentum. Around that six month marker was when I started to rediscover who Zoe was; completely raw, unfiltered, solo Zoe with no strings (or men) attached. This discovery itself turned out to be quite the terrifying challenge as well, as it had been a very long time since I had ever stopped to put myself first, let alone stop to look at the person I had become. This process took a hell of a lot of self-care with manis and pedis coming out my ying-yang. It also took self care in the form of pacing myself, allowing myself to say no or not right now to extra tasks, climbing mountains, saying yes to new adventures, spending some days doing absolutely nothing, and pushing the boundaries of the comfort zone I was so fond of living in.

It wasn't until the end of the Summer of Zoe that I really began to truly discover who Zoe was. And, with that self-discovery came self-love.

Now self-love is never an easy thing to attain, although we all strive for it and hope to succeed in loving ourselves. It doesn't help that the media is always trying to convince us to do better, be better, look better, and feel better. There is always something "wrong" with who we are that makes that self-love unreachable. We're too fat or too thin; we've got too much hair on our legs but not enough on our scalp; we're too outspoken but not assertive enough.

It never seems to end, and each time we're told by someone else that we're not good enough, you can bet we're telling ourselves ten times louder and meaner just how unloveable we are. At least, this has always been the case for me. I am the queen of self-sabotage and self-loathing. I'm fabulous at responding to "you look great" with, "thanks, the sleep-deprived widow look suits me" or "I'm glad I found an outfit to hide a few of my rolls." Someone calls me beautiful, and instead of saying "thank you," I laugh it off or make an incredibly witty comment about something I don't see as perfect on myself.

I see all my flaws dazzling in the spotlight on centre stage for all to see. My tree trunks for thighs; my wide behind speckled with cellulite dots that most definitely could use a back-up cam; my tiger-striped stretch marks spidering up my hips; my round face with a hint of double chin. All my flaws I see highlighted every time I look at myself in the mirror, as if I've just caught an accidental side-view of my naked body while in an uncomfortable position shaving my legs in the bathroom mirror. And, ain't nobody's going to like that view.

Anyway, as you can see, self- love is a tough one for me. And honestly, although I'm learning to love myself, it is definitely still a work in progress. I am; however, learning to take it easier on myself. Learning to be kind to myself and criticize myself less. I am learning to take compliments to heart and say "thank you" more instead of turning compliments into self-inflicted jabs. I am learning to look for the good in myself, praise my accomplishments, and clean my own wounds when I fall. I am learning to love myself first, because I know that I will never be able to love another person again unless I am completely and utterly in love, happy, and proud of myself. I need to love Zoe. Every single roll, stretch mark, and double-chin.

So now what? What does Year Two of Widowhood have in store for me?

•••

"One day you wake up and you're in this place. You're in this place where everything feels right. Your heart is calm. Your soul is lit. Your thoughts are positive. Your vision is clear. You're at peace, at peace with where you've been, at peace with what you've been through, and at peace with where you're headed."

I wish I could say this was me. I wish I could say that the start of Year Two has brought me this peace and that I feel content, happy, and ready to take on my next adventures. But I'm not there yet. In fact, I'm not even close.

Year One was definitely a whirlwind filled with unplanned adventures, tears, panic attacks, wild nights, rough mornings, and plenty of firsts. It was an entirely different year than the year I had planned for months on end. In fact, it was polar opposite of the year I thought was finally going to happen for me. Year One was supposed to be the year I became a mother. And in Quinn's death, that dream died with him too.

Year One was the start of my recovery.

Just the start.

It was a year of rebuild.

Year Two is a fresh start. I have worked hard all year to build a stable base to start my new life on, but there are definitely still a few cracks in this structure. Year Two will be finding out what I need to fill in those cracks so I can continue to build a new future for Zoe. I know Year Two is going to be another challenging year, with plenty more firsts and unexpected hurdles, but I also know I can survive it.

I will survive it.

At some point, I'll stop counting the years post-death. August 31st will eventually become just another day that passes by. One day, the memories won't bring tears. One day, the memories will be just that, memories of a past life, and a beautiful one at that. And I will find peace. I will find my happiness again.

And, one day, whenever that is, I will be called "Mom." And those kids will be the luckiest kids out there. Not because they'll have a bomb-ass, witty-as-hell momma-bear. No, they'll be lucky because they'll have an Uncle Quinn watching their every move and keeping them safe in his arms from above.

I don't believe in much, but that right there, *I just know it.*

Advice to My Past Self, and To Any Other Young Widows Out There

(January 2019)

Reflecting back on my first year as a widow, I have come to realize there were some things I feel I did really well for myself, and some things I wish I could go and have a redo. Year one was a year of firsts, although some might argue some of them weren't truly firsts since it wasn't my first grief rodeo. Still, the grief of a widow compared to the grief of a daughter is nothing alike, and so in many ways, each new experience the year after Quinn died was just as virgin as the first go around with grief.

And, so, as I've been re-reading what I've written in this book, editing and adding as I go, I soon began to realize there was something missing. Yes, I shared my thoughts, opinions, and experiences, but I hadn't really shared my "secrets" of navigating year one, apart from the very obvious wine and chocolate addictions.

So, even though throughout the whole year I was never really eager to take anyone else's advice, here are my "words of wisdom" for getting through Year One of Widowhood:

1. It is perfectly ok to not be ok. Own your grief. Own your sadness. You don't need to put on a "brave face" for anyone. You deserve to grieve what you lost in the way that YOU need to grieve. Don't let anyone else tell you what is right for your grief journey.

   If you need to spend 3 months horizontal on the couch, go for it. If you need to watch sad chick flicks while eating a tub of ice cream each night for 6 weeks straight, by all means do (and for the sake of whoever is "babysitting you," let's hope you're not as lactose intolerant as I am.). If you need to sleep your way through Saskatchewan and drink your way through Alberta, it is *your* life.

   Do whatever gets you through those first few days, weeks, or months. At the start of my first year, I made it very clear to my friends and family that I needed to grieve how I needed to grieve. Yes, at times I got a little out of control, but I always got my control back when the time was right. And, you will too. You deserve a grace period on judgment. When my family and friends voiced their concerns during days when I was in that wild zone, I only said one thing. "If I am doing this a year from now and it is still scaring you, then and only then can you judge me for it and see it as a problem."

I needed that grace period. I needed to find out who I was again. I needed to feel in whatever form I could find feeling in.

And, that was ok.

2. On the same wavelength, don't shame yourself for any of the decisions you have made. Those decisions have kept you alive. They have kept you moving one foot forward to the next, so even if some of them taught you a lesson in a very hard way, guess what? You needed to learn that lesson.

3. Do your best to be present.

My biggest regret of Year One as a widow was focusing only on the milestones. But, honestly, that's how I got through the year. I spent the entire year looking at the calendar and planning when the next big "happy" event would take place.

Going to Florida; the Dominican Republic; England; Thailand. I focused only on those "big events" and saw those as my goals. "Just make it to Florida, Zoe. Then you'll be ok." "Two more weeks to England, and you can breathe again."

In a way, I had to set these goals for myself because so many times I didn't know if I could fight hard enough to get to that next big milestone. I was so overwhelmed with grief and sadness that I didn't see the good in "regular days." I didn't want to be a part of regular days.

What I didn't realize was that those "regular days" were what happiness would stem from. Those little things that happen on those little days truly mean everything. You see, when I think back on the life I led with Quinn, I don't think about the big days often: our wedding, moving to our home in Cochrane, our car accident five days before our high school graduations, my parents deaths... Yes, those were important days, and I do think about them every so often, but they weren't what stand out in my mind about the life Quinn and I shared. No, those big days just came and went without too much day-to-day thought after the initial high passed.

What I do remember from Quinn and Zoe are those little beautiful moments that often seemed quite menial at the time. Quinn pinching my butt when I walked up the stairs in front of him. Quinn sending me silly SnapChats while he sat on the toilet. Going for our evening walks with Layla and judging our neighbours' lawns. Driving in the car together and holding hands over the centre consol.

Honestly, the most vivid of all my Quinn memories was one I never thought would be memorable at all. I remember driving my old Pontiac Vibe with him in the passenger seat. We must have been coming home from Saskatoon, as we had just turned west onto Highway 14 at Wilkie to head back to Unity. One of my favourite songs, "How to Save a Life" by The Fray, had come on the radio, and since I knew every word to the song, I was belting it out Carpool Karaoke-style. I looked over and saw Quinn staring at me with this mesmerized and oh-so-loving look in his eyes. I looked at him and said, "What?!" with a giggle, and he replied, "Wow, you need to sing like that more often. It's beautiful."

The simplest, sweetest memory.

The one that lingers the longest and the strongest; forever etched into my mind. I knew long before that moment he loved me, but holy hell did I feel it most strongly right then and there.

Little tiny day-to-day memories. Those were what counted. Those were what made me love him. Those were what brought happiness to all my days.

And so, it occurred to me that setting goals to get to the big events only made me absent for all the little events. Can I tell you the truth (yet again)? I have almost ZERO recollection of last year apart from what I've written in this book. Seriously, it's a blank chalkboard up in here. I was so focused on surviving to the next "big event" that I completely lost any chance of creating happy memories in between. Now, I know as I write this I'm well past the one-year mark of widowhood, but since this book isn't out yet, I have to share the changes I've made since January 1, 2019 rolled around (marking one and a half years a widow, for those counting).

On January 1st, I realized I needed to make this year a good year for Zoe. No one else could make this a good year for me; I had to choose to make it a good year. So I chose to be present.

What the hell does that mean, Zoe?

It means living in each moment of each day, and finding the happiness in the little things that occur each and every day. Because, at the end of your life (or the end of someone you love's life) you're not going to focus on those "big events." No, you're going to remember those little, tiny, beautiful moments that made that life so special. Those moments create the love. They create the happy.

So, at the beginning of 2019, I made a few changes. I began going to yoga again, to centre myself and find that inner peace, calmness, and the all-powerful "breath." I also started up "Things I Love Thursdays," or TILTs for short, for a second time. For those of you not familiar with TILTs, they are posts I started doing when I was about 16-years-old once a week to reflect on all the good things that happened that week that I am grateful for. Jackie, my supervising officer while I was in Regina in 2009 to get my pilot's license through air cadets, started this tradition by having all the girls contribute to her TILTs each week. TILTs have always been the perfect place to highlight those "little moments" that truly bring the happy to a week for me.

And, for good measure this time around, I also decided to pick one happy memory from the week, write it on a piece of paper, and put it in a jar to open on New Years Eve and reflect on all the happy that happened in that second year of widowhood.

I want to have a good year. I need to have a good year. So, I'm choosing to be present. I'm choosing to create that happy for myself. I'm choosing to live in those little moments. And so far, it feels fucking amazing.

4. Self-care is the highest form of self-love.

Self-care doesn't need to be hoity-toity. Yes, it can involve manicures, pedicures, lash extensions, massages, and shopping sprees; all which are fabulous ways to cope with grief and spend some of that "extra" life-insurance money, by the way; but it can also simply involve getting an extra hour of sleep, soaking in the tub with a good book (or Netflix binge session, as I can honestly say I had absolutely ZERO brain capacity to read a book for about a year after Quinn died), drinking a large mug of peppermint tea, or shutting off all the lights and staring blankly into the darkness for a few hours with your phone on "do not disturb."

It can also be found in the simple act of saying "no." Saying "no" to an extra job at work; saying "no" to a friend wanting to stop by for a visit; saying "no" to a walk with a neighbour; saying "no" to a night out with friends. Some days, you just can't do it. No matter how great the plans are or how much you want to see the person, some days it's just all too damn much. So just fucking say "no."

And, yes, getting in the habit of saying "no" will not be an easy feat at first. I am a notorious "people pleaser," my mom was just as bad as I was, and I truly have a hard time "letting anyone down" or cancelling any plans. But once you start saying "no," I guarantee you are going to start feeling better. Listen to your body. Listen to your mind. If it feels like something is going to be too much for you, guess what? It will be, and the last thing you need is to burn out an already exhausted and brittle body and soul.

Take care of yourself. Be selfish. People will understand. They will be there waiting for you on the sidelines when you're ready to let them in again with big open arms, a shoulder to lean on, and open ears to listen to all your sorrows.

5. Always remember, you are in control of your life.

I firmly believe life is nothing but a series of choices. Many unfortunate things have happened *around* me, but none of them have happened *to* me.

Let me say that again.

Bad things may happen around you,
but they don't happen to you.

You make the decision surrounding
how these events impact you. *You*
can choose to be happy. *You* can
choose to find light in the darkest of
days. *You* can choose to laugh when
every bone in your body is telling
you to cry. Or, *you* can even choose
to cry every single tear you have out,
take a deep breath, and put one foot
in front of the other trying to navigate
your new normal.

These are all your choices to make.
The actions of others, albeit very hard
to deal with at times, should not
dictate the life you live. They should
not alter your self-worth, your zest
for life, or your determination to do
all the beautiful things you plan to
do. Don't let life make you bitter.
Don't let life make your heart hard.
Don't let life eat you up in one big
bite and spit you back onto the
pavement in a puddle of your own
tears. Because at the end of the day,

the only one who is hurting is you.
Do you really want to live that kind
of life?

You deserve a good life, my dear
friend. So choose to live one. Choose
to keep fighting; choose to find
positive in every day; choose to find
yourself; choose laughter; choose
love. Choose to put yourself first.

Then, only then, will you find *your*
happy. And, life will look good
again.

So, hey, girl, hey, guess what?

You've fucking got this.

You are *fierce.*

Epilogue

(October 1, 2018)

"Keep your face to the sunshine and you will not see the shadow."

Today, I am grateful. I made it through September. I made it through the month I have dreaded for months. The month I honestly didn't know if I'd get through. I made it.

Yes, I am exhausted. Yes, there were days where my anxiety skyrocketed and the light was far from my sight, but each night I put myself to bed and told myself there would be a better day in the morning, and I got through it.

Honestly, September wasn't how I pictured it. I thought the worst days would be the first anniversary of Quinn's death and the week following with all the horrid "firsts" coming back into my memory. Instead, those firsts felt beige. Emotionless. My body and mind needed to be numb to survive those few firsts, because I'm not quite ready to face them. And, that's ok.

What surprised me was the fourth anniversary, marking four years without my parents, was the one that hit like a bull crashing through a china shop. A day I thought would be easier than those past turned out to be the toughest, as it was a reminder of just how much I needed to be their little girl this year. How much I craved to lay on their couch and snuggle up with my mommy and daddy. That's what hit the hardest.

But, I got through it. I overcame the sorrow and the panic, the anger and the fear, and September ended.

And, yes, I'm very aware it's just a date on a calendar. It's just another month in a year. I'm also very aware I could have plenty of hard days in October or November, or any other month really. But right now, I honestly feel like the weight I've been carrying all month has finally been lifted, and I can breathe again. I see the light, and I know I can continue to overcome.

I see you shining, Babe, and you're the
brightest star in my sky. Stay with me; you
know you're always needed.

Now, excuse me while I sleep for two days.

•••